METANOIA

Also by Mari Perron

Memoria: The Way of the Marys

Mirari: The Way of the Marys

A Course of Love

The Given Self

Creation of The New

Peace: Book 3 of The Grace Trilogy

Love: Book 1 of The Grace Trilogy
with Julianne Carver and Mary Kathryn Love

Metanoia

Book III of

The Way of the Marys

From A COURSE OF LOVE's First Receiver

MARI PERRON

A Dialogue on Mary of Nazareth's Way of Mary

Copyright 2025 by Mari Perron
All rights reserved.
First Edition 2025

No part of this book may be used or reproduced in any form or by any means, electronic or mechanical, including photocopying, recording, or by any information storage and retrieval system, without permission in writing from the publisher.

Course of Love Publications
432 Rehnberg Place
St. Paul, MN 55118
Library of Congress Cataloguing-in-Publishing Data
Perron, Mari
Metanoia: The Way of the Marys

ISBN: 978-0-9728668-9-7
Creation, Spirituality, The Feminine, Time, Alchemy, Prophecy, Mysticism, The New
Cover Design by Terry Widner and Abbie Phelps
Editor: Michael Mark

DEDICATION

To you, the reader ...

may you view yourself kindly, and me too.

Such loving kindness awakens us to one another.

Together,

From the heart of ourselves

We may heal the heart of the world.

M

Contents

Invocation	11
The Decade: 2020	12

INTRODUCTION

A Revolution in Consciousness	15
The Incoming	16
The Weavers Will Come	17

THE INCOMING BEGINS

The Surprising Commencement of Metanoia	21
The Women in Philadelphia	23
The Second Movement and the Continuing Impact	25
The Choiceless Choice	27
The Birth of Our Way of Marys	30

THE OPENING OF THE NEW

Metanoia is Chaos	35
Starting Anew	36
The Vision of The New	37
What is Metanoia?	40
Metanoia's Dialogue of Liberation	45
New Creation	47
Chaos	52
The Open Door of Hope	55

Where Something Happens	57
The First Act: Holy Relationship	59
When a Calling Finds You Endings Follow	62
Callings	65
The Prophetic	68
Vulnerability and the Movements It Inspires	72
Creative Lives Express Another Way	74
2014 Encounters	76

THE IMPOSSIBLE MEETS THE POSSIBLE

The Return	81
Metanoia: The Great Turning	82
The Great Turning... in Time	84
The Dim	87
Soul	88
Light and Soul	89
Anima Mundi: The World Soul	91
Wonderings: In and Within the Dark	94
The Girl in the Velcro Dress	96

2020: A TIME OF TRANSFORMATION

The Start of the Pandemic	103
The Wound of the Womb	106
Let Yourself Feel Loved	112
Breaking Free Is the End of Learning	115
Daily Reverie	118
Transfiguration	124
Couplings	128
Receive Instead of Plan	129

Ripening	131
Revelation Is Your Heritage	133
Revelation Is Knowing Shared	135

THE POWER OF BEING

Breaking the Barriers of Conventional Knowing: Being Affected	139
The Support that Didn't Come	145
A Revolution that Honors the Pain	147
The Legacy of Trauma and My Return to Voice	149
Pronouncements and Their Effects	157
Being a Birth Mother	164
Feeling for Yourself	166
The Way of Mary: Breaking the Chain / Going Elsewhere	169
Use and Energy	172

CLOSING OUT THE OLD

Fragility and Lace	177
Quietude	180
Fulfillment and Desire	182
The New Orbit	184
Lace and the Feminine	186
Taking a New Turn: The Brain	190
Sharing Spaciousness	191
The Twin Whirlwinds and the Infinity of Time	193
Wholehearted Freedom	199
Wholeness	200
Surrendering to the Current of The New	202
Flashes	205

Time Outside of Time Is Finding Us	206
What is the Transition? Surrender to the New	207
Like the Moon	210
Being Truly Choiceless	211
Non-Linear Time	214
The Sabbatical	216
The Cross of Time and Space	219
Ensoulment of the World	222
The Dynamic	223
The Power to Imagine	224
Fragility	226
A Tribe of Personified Being	228
A Way of Reflection	230
The New Is the Challenge of Every Age	232

THE SECOND COMING: LIFE AS IT'S SELF

Metanoia: Revolution, Revelation & Reality	237
Recouping the Loss of Holy Relationship Through Creation of The New	241
Knowing With	243
The Third-Something and Holy Relationship	244
The Soul Returns Home	247
The End of Defense & Lamentations	248
The Beyond Within	250
Epiphany	251
Do Not Look for Cause	253
Taking on the Same Nature	255
The Incoming	257
The All of Everything & the Void of Nothing	260
The Promise of the Spacious Self	264

Waking Dreams & Metanoia's Internal Revolution	268
Love's Sweetness: In Recovery	272
Realization of the Revelation	279
A New Genesis: Twoness	280
Epilogue, 2024: As You Begin to Trust You Begin to Extend Who You Are	283
Dedication	286
Answers to My Prayers and Gratitude for My People	288
Reference Guide and Related Works	292

Invocation

Our Holy Ones do not often choose their messengers from among the . . . "fine." Jesus, and now Mary, take in the walking wounded, the hard cases, the troubled hearts.

For the healing of the heart.
As we heal our hearts, we are healing the world.
Blessed Mary came . . . to me and to us.
She came "back" to us.
She is one of us.
She lived. She birthed. She hurt. She healed.
She went all the way down before she rose.
Then she came back to us, to be for us.
For us and our counterpart Mother Earth.

The Decade

2020

We are close now, close to a time in which a new choice can make true living available here and now. This is the decade in which transformation proceeds, and the time in which the mother's heart enters to show the way to care for the living, and realize the end of what does not need to be.

This is the time of Metanoia: The Way of the Marys.

M

INTRODUCTION

A REVOLUTION IN CONSCIOUSNESS

As the "son of God" came to anchor the truth of who you are into consciousness, (one in being with God), so the "daughters of God"* now are called upon to honor the fulfillment of the way of Jesus with the passing into The New, the new age that we are calling "The Way of the Marys." This is a move from the masculine to the feminine of time, an anchoring of the infinite awareness of the consciousness of creation . . . in time. As ordinal time is left behind, we weave time together with time outside of time, birthing time's awareness of itself as helpmate to human fulfillment and extension—through spaciousness, into spaciousness.

---

* In 1998, as I sat at my dining room table sharing coffee with Mary Love, she told me of her dream of "a new *Course in Miracles*," and I shared with her that I had awoken to, "You and Mary will have something to do with the end of ordinal time." See *Mirari* p. 273, also 130-31

The Incoming

"This is about what 'comes to you,' " Holy Mary says.

"Oh yes. I do know about that," I reply.

She calls me "well practiced," and tells me, "You have written to the end of limited space, and the way of writing in spaciousness has opened for you.

"You are done now with the prescribed. Done with the ordered. You are writing with the incoming. Not beforehand. Not after. In the coming. We are the incoming. We are the incoming tide of The New. We, the women, are now the bringers of the Word."

The Weavers Will Come

A Course of Love

[A]vailability is what is meant by the anchoring of the new. Those who, in relationship with the unknown, through unity and imagination, create the new by means other than doing, open a way previously unknown, and as all forerunners do, anchor that way within consciousness by holding open this door to creation. They, in truth, create a new pattern and begin to weave it into the web of reality, anchoring it for discovery by their brothers and sisters.

Mirari: The Way of the Marys, Book I

There is a bond between the reader and the Word, especially these Holy Words. There is a bond between all creative partners. It is a needed bond. It acknowledges the weaving together of the art and its manifestation.

Memoria: The Way of the Marys Book II

The undoing is what you were once so impacted by in the *Course* chapter on Oneness and Duality. But now the "possibility" of light is the "presence" of light. This light joins in the swirl of energy that continues to unravel the threads of time. This is happening very gently. And then... then dear one... the weavers will come to create the new time.

Metanoia: The Way of the Marys Book III

Incarnation is the miracle taking place in time. Seeing-through connects to what you can imagine in the view of your feelings and in the lace that overlays them. This is the intricate and beautiful web of The New. Here, with the tiny point of a needle, we begin to see the weaving together of truth and feelings.

The Incoming Begins

The Surprising Commencement of Metanoia (That I Didn't See at the Time)

In March of 2013, the same year in which I first heard from Mother Mary,* an astrologer friend, Pat Kaluza, told me that what people want from me is for me to take care of them. Because we met only infrequently, she could see this by watching the unfolding of my life from one year to the next. And as an astrologer, she could see these tendencies in my stars. I knew in my heart that she was right... and I knew how much care I'd given that was a mistake. In one way this feeling of concern was a trait of mine, an innate part of my nature, a way of being. In another, it was a destructive pattern.

It was my relationship with care-giving that led me to begin to explore feminism in my favored way: through reading and writing. I read on feminism voraciously and began to write a book I tentatively called *Discovering Feminism in the Canning Room*, because that is what happened: I rediscovered feminism as I cleaned the basement room where my old books were stored.

Feminism was "in me" all along but I found it there in the basement, tucked away with the Christmas ornaments and the manger, alongside Halloween decorations and board games, one shelf removed from the canning jars. It was not so much "thought about" as it was just there in the background, in the proverbial underground of my psyche. As it made its way out of the damp and

---

* see *Mirari*, p. 13

dark, and moved into the light, it entered that middle space where heart eludes the mind.

How amazing that it first emerged as the ancient and yet prophetic image of the women on their haunches before a fire, protecting the new babe from the wild dogs.

When I rediscovered this opening, I was terribly perplexed. How had I forgotten it? But I knew the cause. I had been in the midst of protecting a literal new babe, my grandson, and in my literalism hadn't realized that the new babe was also me.

Now, I know the part that belongs to Metanoia's revolution. It is coming out of the dark consciousness that obscures, to the consciousness of light that illuminates. The Christ-light. Having explored our path, we're left to connect the dots, follow our tracks to their destination, and claim our new lives.

When our Holy Ones "reach out" to us, and we know it, the New path has already come, the choiceless choice has been made. Here, it has become apparent for all the babes of The New.

We have entered Metanoia's revolution of consciousness.

The Women in Philadelphia

An invitation from the Center for Contemporary Mysticism in Philadelphia was the start. It was the spring of 2018 and I was to join Jon Mundy[*] at an event featuring both *A Course in Miracles* and *A Course of Love*. Mary Love[†] spoke along with me for the first time.

When the conference was over, she and I met with three women whom I was graced to know from a previous visit to the Center—Rhetta Morgan, Jackie Lesser, and Helen Burke—at Helen's home. Mary set a camera on a tripod to record our dialogue. In the midst of the gentle sharing, I had a breakdown, of which Mother Mary would soon say to me, "*There, in a small group of women, there was recognition of the time of 'the Marys' coming into being . . . without fuss.*"[‡]

At the time, Holy Mary said, "*One does not know the unknown they are bringing into being in the same way one knows the hatching of a plan. It is more as if, unknowingly, the idea is held in suspension. It has been spoken. It has been heard. Its time of fullness will be revealed.*"[§]

When I returned from Philadelphia and began to feel the first prompts to expand the Way of Mary, they quickly grew into their time of fullness. I wrote in my journal: "Good Lord, I'm seeing that maybe we've been moving all this time to enter the intertwined

---

[*] Jon Mundy is a reverend, author, friend, and ACIM leader.

[†] Mary Love is my soul sister of over 30 years.

[‡] *Mirari*, p. 273

[§] *Mirari*, p. 274

circles* of the Way of Jesus and the Way of Mary. To come to hold that inner circle in ourselves, and stand outside of the world—in the world." Being reminded of this through the sharing we did was more than impactful. So were the words of a song Helen and Rhetta had prepared to share with us called "The Great Turning." It kept going through my mind:

"In this great turning, we will learn to lead in love."†

By August 4th, Mary Love was nearly finished editing the recording she had made during our visit. Because of my vulnerability, I'd asked her to change a few things. When this was done, she invited me over to view it again and was brimming with happiness. It was the first time I spoke of the Way of Mary,‡ but not as something "coming." I said, "It's calling me."

---

* *ACOL* D:Day19.16

† Lyrics by Karisha Longaker of MaMuse.

‡ The Way of Mary was first announced in "The Dialogues" of *A Course of Love* as representing incarnation through relationship, demonstrating the truth of union, the birth of form, and the ascension of the body. See *ACOL* D:Day17.10

The Second Movement and the Continuing Impact

The second movement of this new beginning within me started with the twentieth anniversary of *A Course of Love*'s commencement. The idea of a December conference to celebrate its inception (December 1, 1998) was conceived by a lovely Scottish man, James Kelly. This heartened me and I took a sabbatical to prepare. Part of this was compiling an archive of those twenty years ... one that I could just sit with. Be with. I loved it. It was my "one thing."

My review brought aspects of those two decades into greater fullness. But it did more than that. When I was nearly done, I felt I had settled back into the ground of my being. I wrote in my journal that, "I can feel myself coming to a lovely completion of that gift of the past, a past that's been carried into a new future. I now feel like I have all my sweet chicks gathered safely in the hen house. This is my treasure of fact and memory, of the world and of me and of Jesus, of a near twenty-year relationship—sweet and feisty, profound and casual, tough and gentle, giddy and solemn, and above all loving and personal."

A final piece came as I was reading and appreciating the Mary Magdalene book by Cynthia Bourgeault,* in which she speaks of the "crucible of transformation" and of how "sticking with human

---

* Bourgeault, Cynthia. *The Meaning of Mary Magdalene: Discovering the Woman at the Heart of Christianity.* Shambhala, 2010, p. 218.

intimate partnership through all that happens, brings this transformation to its fruition."

These readings became revelations. The mention of "human intimate partnership" (with the divine) by such an insightful author allowed me to feel what an incredible privilege it is to do what I'm doing and to have the freedom to stay on the path that calls me, even when it changes. To know "this," not "that" is what I am to do . . . because I trust myself and my inspiration. Me and my Holy Ones and a dozen or so "have my back" people. I felt that all that had happened was beginning to see the light of day in me. All the movements, the feelings, and the trials.

I was accepting, for the first time, that this creative relationship with my Holy Ones is also a vocation. The realization sparked a journey of remembrance and review of this period in my life. A time of remembering, freely feeling, exploring, and researching ensued. I was both thrilled and calm at the same time. I gained a renewed sense of the breadth of my experience.

In late August, I discovered I had contracted Lyme disease. This gave me another reason to rest, and in that month, I found a narrative I'd written about the beginning of *A Course of Love* on old disks, printed it, and read it lying on the couch. This, too, had an effect on me. I wrote: "It feels amazing to me that I have landed where I have without a plan. I am thrilled and calm at the same time."

Then on Wednesday, August 6th I went to Mary Love's to see her video.

THE CHOICELESS CHOICE

When I got home from Mary's I addressed Jesus, telling him, "Mary has redone the 'healing' video, and talked to you, my Brother, and read me her dialogue with you. She was so happy with seeing me, and me her, that we spoke of continuing to share on Wednesdays into infinity. Then we watched the video of us in Philadelphia, and one of Sarah Bareilles, where she sings about choice and freedom. And I confided to Mary that, for the first time in my life, I'm feeling free to choose in a way that feels choiceless . . . because 'I know.' "

Then I found these words coming out of my mouth, "I feel that I might be about to begin something on the Way of Mary." I'd not before admitted this, even to myself.

I became anxious to reread my printed copy of "Subjective Religious Experience," which was the first substantial piece I'd written after *ACOL* was complete. I'd re-found it while preparing for the conference. But I knew not to read that either, because it was more of the mind, and I wanted to write something of the heart and of this feeling of the power of our voices in this time. Power for good. Power for The New. Womanly power. I was still feeling disempowered by the republication of *ACOL*, as if everything that I'd been holding close had been taken out of my hands. I had sought publishing and was glad for the new readership, yet felt I had lost my place in it, and so somehow had lost my Self. I was searching for that Self again and hoped to come back to what I knew to be the significance of my experience.

I realized how often Jesus had coached me in those twenty years to go the "time-saving" way of giving up difficulties, and how I almost never took that option, and so all the years . . . were years spent in conflict and worry and recovery. And I declared:

"I don't want that anymore! I want the Miracle and its time-saving properties. I want to live the Miracle. I want to give birth to The New and I want to birth the Way of Mary. I really do. What's in 'The Dialogues' is simply not enough and too mild. It's like something's missing, and somehow, I'm missing too. And maybe I've had to feel the choice as my own, and that I'm free, before I could admit to it. I don't know if it's up to me at all, but I suspect that it is, and is in a way far greater than I realize. I can be an open heart letting love flow into the world again. If you want me to."

It was only then that the prophecy from 2013 returned to my awareness. Mother Mary had come to me, then, with a radical message that I recorded and soon forgot. The publication of *A Course of Love*'s combined volume was just getting underway, and at the same time my husband and I were investing ourselves in caring for my daughter and her child, our grandson.

Later, it became clear just how perfect that combination was. Protecting both daughter and grandchild brought up more fierce mother love than I'd ever experienced. It joined with Mother Mary's impassioned call to focus on "the She of humanity":

Now it is like Mother Earth. Lead you into yourself. Plant your own seeds in your own soil. You are the seed and the soil as is She. The She of humanity. Now plant what gives back to yourself as She begins to plant what gives back to Herself, her living body. She is responding. Listen to her Roar.*

---

* *Mirari*, p. 13

That early visitation from Mother Mary only rarely came to mind, until the events of 2018, when the need for stability of both my daughter and grandson opened me to "receive instead of plan." This was one of my major insights from *A Course in Miracles*: "Today we will receive instead of plan, that we may give instead of organize."*

This line from *ACOL* reinforced it: "To be willing to receive instead of plan is to break the pattern of planning."†

---

* *ACIM Original Edition* W1:135.23, scribed by Helen Schucman
† *ACOL* T3:22.5

The Birth of Our Way of Marys

Since the first day I sat ready to enter the Way of Mary, I anchored myself by writing in my journal. It became my practice . . .

. . . There is a morning glory in the woods. I've never seen one here before. Wouldn't it be lovely if they were to spread and populate the ground around me? I keep dreaming of what flowers might be started on this rough patch, yet there is something about the wildness and mess that I like. I have to admit it. There's nothing like it anywhere else, except maybe on an old farmer's land where there's a jumble of living things, and things left behind, and the creeping, leafy things taking over.

At 7:12 the first squirrel sits on Mademoiselle Maple,* one eye pointed toward me, one the other away—as is the way of the squirrel! From the way of the squirrel, I go to that first introduction to the Way of Mary from 2013 and find that its astounding nature fills me with hope and . . . almost a sort of dread of beginning again . . . until I get to the end and read:

Do not let this take you over. This must come in the way of dialogue. You are to be part of it. My son and I have heard your anguish and we include you here, along with us, in relationship with us, to reveal your true heart.†

---

* My miracle tree that graced the cabin for years before needing to be taken down, and that then regrew out of her trunk.

† *Mirari*, p. 20

This brought up such great longing in me that I said, "Please do help me, Mother and Brother, to reveal my true heart. I know the turnaround you are inspiring is beyond teaching and learning, and that's where I've wanted to be since the possibility was first mentioned. Now, I feel it's where I've landed."

That original mention of moving beyond learning came when I was receiving the "Fourth Treatise: A Treatise on the New." It was the only one I didn't share as it came.[*] It began on November 1, 2000, and on the 9th, an offer to publish "The Course" of *A Course of Love* arrived from New World Library. My literary partner of the time,[†] Dan Odegard, began to engage with the publisher's representative, Marc Allen, and I felt totally free to receive this treatise without engagement with the group. I loved giving it my full and undivided attention . . . and what was more, my passion surged as Jesus spoke of the end of the old way of learning and the beginning of creation of The New.

The thrust of this treatise is the union of the human and the divine. Jesus links it to the end of learning, to a change in our way of coming to know, and to our becoming creators of The New:

[T]here is no need for teachers or for learners. There is need only for the sustainability of Christ-consciousness in which we exist together as creators in unity and relationship.[‡]

---

[*] Early on, there was a group I met with regularly to share portions of *ACOL* as they were received.

[†] Dan Odegard, a friend and former literary agent whom I'd known from before I began receiving *A Course of Love*, took an interest in supporting me and promoting the book from the very beginning.

[‡] *ACOL* T4:11.3

The future depends on you who are willing to leave learning behind and who are willing to accept your new roles as creators of the new—creators of the future.*

"A Treatise on The New" was completed in exactly one month. The treatise ends with a description of "our new means of communicating and creating, a *sharing* that replaces learning with what is beyond learning." Jesus invites us to be, along with Him, "creators of the future through the sustainability of Christ-consciousness."†

Returning to Holy Mary, I say, "Who we each are uniquely can't be truly represented with anything other than our lives: our humanity, our hearts, feelings, voices, the depth of our longing and desire, and the places where that longing and desire is met. *A Course of Love*, the Way of Jesus, and the Way Mary—they aren't teachings but a joining in relationship—a transformative relationship."

... And then our Way of Mary began.

... And now, as we conclude Mary's way with Metanoia, I realize: The Great Turning is the end of learning, and the end of learning is the dissolution of the old and the commencement of Metanoia's revolution for, and of, The New.

---

* *ACOL* T4:11.2
† see *ACOL* T4:11.2-5

The Opening of the New

METANOIA IS CHAOS

Metanoia is chaos. I'm going through it. This is a breakdown.

STARTING ANEW

Receiving and writing *Metanoia* felt like the most challenging thing I'd ever been through.

Then I started my review...

I finally asked myself, "How can you see clearly when you're 'in it'?" I wondered if I'd been in Metanoia's chaos all along. "Is that why I've been struggling so?"

I didn't admit to this inner chaos until I was well into my second or third round of review, each needed because I couldn't remember what I'd read the previous time. All I knew at this point was the impact of starting anew each day. And the next day forgetting what I'd done the day before. It was very trying. But...

Starting anew is the way of Metanoia.

The Vision of the New

Beginning again by getting back to "us" Mary, my first insight may be finding that many have already made a break with the old—whatever that is for each of us. And the thing is, with the sympathetic understanding that is offered in these books of ours, we can heal from our old wounds, which, in effect, releases us from the past without dismissing one single thing as irrelevant to our arrival in a new present.

We may never forget the reasons for our pain or the wrongs that caused us to lose ourselves, but by feeling the throbbing discomfort of our grief over our long-delayed recognition of "who we are," we are not only liberated from those burdens but freed to make a new rhythm out of that old dirge. What I found is that this is when I became an agent of this revolutionary change. I "knew" it was so when I couldn't, absolutely couldn't, go back for more of the same. I had moved on. When we've moved on, we're in The New and there is nothing left to forgive because everything that's happened to us has brought us to The New.

We then live in amazement, in awe of finding that our lives matter for reasons other than, and greater than, we've seen. When we know this, we know we're heading somewhere New.

It may be a time of recognizing the vision and the wisdom that only comes of being who you are to be "here," and the sense that if you're "fully here" you'll find a way to express who you are here to "be." As you and I accept all, rather than just some of our feelings, we discover the power of creation that rests within them and in the spaces between thought and feeling—between the past, and a future yet to come. We find we've been made eager to enter unknown knowing.

"Here" we move from what was revealed, into the awareness that the revelation has occurred. The revelation has occurred. It is real. The new time has come to be and can be chosen . . . now.[*]

This shift to my own idea of how we "know," first came in the beautiful Chapter 20 of *A Course of Love*, entitled "The Embrace":

This is the first transition, the transition in which you really "get it" that the unknown cannot be taught, laid out on a map, or shown to you by another.[†]

That little sentence holds an essential piece of the wisdom of The New. From it, I discovered the great gift of knowing that no one could tell me (or you) how to achieve a new state of being. The operative, or inoperative word here is "achieve," but "telling" isn't much better.

Mary's way, and our feminine way, will not "tell" you to "achieve" anything. It lets us slow down and realize that the idea of following a plan toward a set goal is obsolete. The predicted end of learning has arrived. How could it not, in a new age that is being created as we live it? How can we navigate it if we follow an old blueprint? Our own eagerness to leave the old behind is the propellant of what is called "a true ending"—an ending within us and within our reality. A true end of learning comes with the inception of vision.

---

[*] *Mirari*, p. 308

[†] *ACOL* D:Day20.3

All of this is a measure of our sovereignty as knowing beings. Here, with that ascendent liberation from conventional knowing, we are endowed with the freedom to create The New.

A benefit of achievement's falling away is the spaciousness it frees up within us. An inner chamber is readied. We make room for the "literal" birth of The New in us, as us.

Relief from use and achievement frees us of external goals. Realizing there's no path to follow, potential is ready to find us in a way that does not allow it, or us, to be used.* This blessed path to The New is being shown to us by Mary of Nazareth, a woman, a mother, and a deity who knows what it is to birth The New into being.

---

* See Chapter 9 of *ACOL*, paragraphs 43 and 44 on use and abuse.

What is Metanoia?

Metanoia is a revolution in consciousness.

This book explores that revolution, the way revolution and revelation go together, and the wonder that comes of having a consciousness that is *still* (and always) coming into its fullness.

Even when it's only an idea.

A word. One word. *Metanoia.*

It started working on me right away.

Why do some words speak to us and others not? Is it really due to right timing, as I've been thinking it is? How does our consciousness experience a revolution? What would that look like?

I felt that this exploration would take being present to what is most alive in me, to what makes me . . . me. And as soon as I had that thought, I got pretty excited. For me and for you.

What a wonder it's been to have a word-idea take on a life of its own. Metanoia began asking, right away, that I pay attention, and that was about it.

I started out in the classic way of seeing what's been said about Metanoia, mainly because I had a vague memory of it from decades ago when I found James Hillman and fell in love with his way of speaking. Somehow, this way was captured in his writing. Encountering his one-of-a-kind voice is a bit like being run over by a truck. Why any of us like such feelings of high impact is a mystery. But I did.

I loved him without understanding, and felt I got the gist of what he was saying through some kind of writerly magic akin to what happens as I receive from my Holy Ones. It's taken me a long time to admit it, and to see this writing I've been doing in the same light. But I've realized my writings with Jesus and Mary have been an equally hard-hitting experience, and I find that to be full of wonder.

Like most souls, I only continue to ponder those ideas that I feel matter—to contemplate words that mean something to me even if I don't know why. When I persist like this, without knowing why, an opening for new knowing often emerges.

Although I knew of Metanoia in the 90's, I'd not heard of Metanoia from one "current" book as I began this work. Now I'm hearing more of it. Why is Metanoia finding increased attention in this 2020 decade? What is making it new ... again?

I see Metanoia as a great blessing and change agent, come to push out the old so that a New "time of no time"* can commence. This "new time of no time" was first mentioned in *A Course of Love*'s chapter on The Embrace, which itself was the aftereffect of realizing that the solution to oneness and duality is transformation.

Metanoia *is* the transformation.

This had a great impact on me, even when it was only an "idea" of transformation. But then the idea took on a life of its own. I feel it's done so because of the relationship it has to my soul, and our souls. My soul, our souls, only continue to wonder about things that matter—that mean something to us—even if we don't know what that "something" is, maybe especially when we don't know.

My guess, now, after spending a couple of years with Metanoia, is that it works a miracle in us by remaining undefined. It intrigues us simply by bringing the indescribable into greater prevalence. We've

---

* "The time of parables has ended. A new time of no time awaits. Nothing is like unto anything else. Likeness, like thingness, has been overcome with oneness. Oneness prevails. The reign of Christ is at hand." *ACOL* C:20.13. See also *ACOL* T2:6.1, D:5.21, D:Day16.9.

lived in a known world and time, and now we are facing a move into a new and unknown world, one that is encouraging us to rediscover newness in what we haven't seen all along.

It was Metanoia's very *unfamiliarity* that captured me, even when I succumbed to exploring the hints and clues that pointed me in the direction of "getting it." It was only in light of my own experiences—experiences that were also quite vague in the "definition" department—that I realized I need the undefinable as the background for my revolution of consciousness. (One that's been underway for a while.) And I believe you will too. If we're not open to what we don't yet know, The New can't arrive.

M

I return to my old books so often that my renewed interest in James Hillman isn't surprising. That he'd also caught the attention of the scholar and author Tom Cheetham called me to him as well. Cheetham is, to me, today's rendition of that same kind of intellectual and soulful power that Hillman evidenced. But only now has my interest, really my love for them—(I tend to fall in love with writers)—begun to feel less obscure to me. What I've come to understand is that I need them, too, in the background of my own revolution of consciousness.

I attended a group Cheetham led to explore Hillman's work, so I did engage with him. Afterwards I sent him a copy of *Mirari*. But I think works that are classified as channeling, or inspired writing, even though I usually speak of mine as "received writing," have not yet found much scholarly interest, even in those scholars who explore such happenings of the past.

Although I'm going to cite some "meanings," I feel that meaning isn't the "be all/end all" anymore. It's for this reason that I share my "experience," experience largely based on feelings and encounters.

M

One "definition" of Metanoia that is offered *is* as a "revolution," and one of the meanings of revolution is of a "turn around." So, some definitions went well with what I knew, and what Mother Mary suggests. They're valuable for pointing us in a new direction.

In a way, this direction sprung itself on me. At 2020's end, *Mirari* was published and I began to edit *Memoria*. But I was soon receiving *Metanoia* as well. I knew little more about it than that it concerned a change of *mind* that changes *us* . . . that causes us, quite without our volition . . . to turn "around" so to speak, or to look back as well as forward to see what we hadn't seen before.

Exploring, I saw "metanoia" translated as repentance (which can have a negative connotation), but then found that John Calvin looked at repentance as "laying aside the old and putting on a new mind" . . . also a theme of these dialogues.

Additionally, I became aware that Metanoia is described as a "change" of mind, a conversion, and a transformative change of heart. James Hillman used Mary's exact words for it: *a revolution of consciousness*. Hers was the call I couldn't ignore, and it all suits the contents of the exploration that I feel this work to be. We're each a pioneer of "inner" experiences that come of looking for a way to bring our full nature to the living of our lives and our creation of The New.

Finally, Metanoia is also associated with Transfiguration. The setting on the mountain, along with the event of humans meeting with God, brought the temporal and the eternal together as one. This event adds a dimension to Metanoia, as well as a new way of seeing "the mountain top" experience of "The Dialogues" of *A Course of Love*. Metanoia could, in that way, describe and expand all that Jesus began, and Mary continues now.

My sense of it is that Metanoia concerns everything that's possible that we haven't known is possible. And it comes by way of our desire to create The New and to "be" the new creation that is on its way into being. I'm not talking with any hesitation when I say "my sense of it." All we can do is "sense" what is yet to come.

It took what I'll call the "experience" of Metanoia to relieve me of my own need for the old order. You'll see this as I share encounters blessed to my psyche, but often confusing and uncomfortable for both my body and mind.

As Mother Mary suggests, this is a liberation movement, and I was about to discover my need for liberation. This is what I share "as it happened." Most of my dialogues with Mary came very naturally as I sat in my backyard cabin, writing within the intimacy of my journal.

Metanoia's Dialogue of Liberation

As Mother Mary and I began, she described Metanoia as "an orbiting revolution that encircles the thinking mind and frees it from what it has been and the use it has been put to."*

The greatest of scientists, psychologists, and theologians experienced Metanoia. Their consciousness accepted the "swirl" of new knowing that moved them beyond what they could use their thinking minds to attain to the basis of all discovery. They imagined what could not yet be imagined. Opening your consciousness to The New is all that is needed. That's the door set ajar. Freedom of the imagination relieves your mind of its restriction and takes you through the open space that is the entrance to the unknown. All that imagination seeks lies beyond the "already" known. Being liberated from the "use" of knowledge is not only your revolution but the end of use. Only the already known can be used.

Metanoia will liberate you from your own tyranny and the lack of freedom that has come from use become abuse:

From the simple concept of individuals needing to be in relationship to survive has grown [a] complex web of use and abuse.†

---

* Throughout this book, Mary's voice is presented in italics.

† *ACOL* C:9.43

Use, in any form, leads to bondage, and so to perceive a world based on use is to see a world where freedom is impossible.*

Abuse is but improper use.†

"Your revolution in consciousness" Mary told me, *"keeps you from being used."*‡

The truth is that Holy works cannot be used. Those who would seek to use them toward specific ends will find themselves thwarted.

Metanoia speaks of expanded consciousness because it is a shared consciousness. Are you willing to recognize that you inhabit a shared consciousness? Can you begin to sense it? And that it is a manner of being in which no use is involved . . . ever. There is not more than one shared consciousness, so there can never be a consciousness that uses or one that is being used. A shared consciousness has no divisions. Here, as with all other separations perpetuated by an either/or way of thought that includes the notion of "use or be used" you will find that as these divisions collapse, your idea of the "reality" of a separate Heaven and Earth (or separated realms) will also fade. Once this happens, each one's revolution begins. You become conscious of the multiplicity of Heaven and Earth's life . . . in you . . . and each of your sisters and brothers.

---

* *ACOL* C:9.43

† *ACOL* C:9.44

‡ Holy Mary also said that, as the first receiver of *A Course of Love*, I was not "used," and that I hadn't "used" what I received. I received *A Course of Love* from Jesus over a period of three years. It began at the end of 1998 and was made up of three books, The Course, The Treatises, and The Dialogues, originally published separately. Jesus delivered the work as "a new Course in Miracles."

New Creation

In a recent dialogue with Jesus, I claimed my weakness, saying, "It's like I fall back on weakness as soon as I have help."

Jesus said, **Is that what you think you do? Go from strong to weak? Is that why you keep working hard when you don't have to? And work 'harder' than you have to?**[*]

Mari, do you feel weak accepting my help?

Sort of. I feel weak, or soft with the tears that rise as I feel your presence, and even more poignant, is the feeling that you "care" for me.

I do, and I can be your strength if you let me be. "Your" strength.

Even strength of mind, Jesus?

Even strength of mind.

M

There was a time, my sister, when you realized the creative connection between yourself and Michael Mark[†] at a deeper level. It is a connection in the imaginal realm where creation of The New is taking place. It feels like a long time ago because realizations stand outside of time, and once come, reveal that they have always been present. Our Mother understands and has supported your connection with him.

---

[*] Throughout this book, Jesus's voice is presented in bold text.

[†] Michael is a "writing friend" with whom I've enjoyed many conversations about creativity, self-expression and the possible.

Mary joins us and says, *Michael lives in your memory, as do his words. Do you see? We wish for all to realize the symmetry between the connection that is "union with" and "memory." They are not the same, but they also are not different. Your memory of me is the same as your union with me. What you receive of me is more than words, it is Memoria. It is Mirari. It is Metanoia.*

When we (Jesus and I) enter union with you as creators of The New, there comes to be a unity of creative truth that is not "about" anything but the union, which is the place of meeting, the place in-between. Now that you know it's there, it is complete.

You do not have to invoke it. Because you are aware, the sense of awareness fades. It is existent . . . always there. That trust continues to live in each of you and to open the natural knowing that has been concealed in the realm of effort and the idea of being singular—capable only of a particular knowing.

As you have known continuously, when you become one in the union of friendship, this trust is also apparent. Shared knowing has been true for you in Holy Relationships. The trust you gain from these can help bring out what has held you back.

This that we do, is a "way" that is true for you "as a writer" in a manner much like it is true for your beloved Father Adrian* "as a priest." Once the vocational breakthrough of a calling occurs it's nearly impossible to go back. A great effort at denial can cause delay, but it is done. A calling can't be thwarted without loss of soul. With acceptance of a call, you become creators in union and relationship . . . which doesn't mean you get organized or do the same

---

* Fr. Adrian was my dear parish priest for decades. He died December 1, 2024, as this book was being prepared for publication. He enlarged our hearts for decades and is deeply missed.

work. It is more that you will be prepared to share the chaos of Metanoia, to speak of it in your own ways, and to create from it Your New as well as The New.

This book has been your greatest challenge yet. You and Christie* have gone through this crucible to reach Metanoia together. The crucible has been about death, grief, aging, the loss of parts of Self that you treasured, memories you would rather hadn't returned, and perplexing challenges to what was known in memory . . . before you began to know newly.

This is the beginning. New knowing takes you out of the "old" chaos to the new chaos.

The new chaos is that of Metanoia. Metanoia is now your change agent.

Here, you go through the chaos of facing your "hardest thing." The change that is particular to your revolution of consciousness. This is different than facing a fear. This is about moving through "the deepest, darkest chaos of your mind" to embrace what has been lost, primarily the loss of who you once knew yourself to be: how you knew yourself to be in relationship with those you love, with those you feared, with those who silenced you or troubled you, and with those who inspired and welcomed you. This is about what has had the greatest effect on you. For Christie it was the loss of her partner, Pam, with whom she felt complete—whole. Loss of wholeness is the major change agent of Metanoia.

For you, the chaos has been amplified in the writing of Metanoia herself. The she of Metanoia arrived, not with Metanoia "as a subject" but within Metanoia "as an actuality," a presence, and an experience

---

* Christie Lord and I met when she was a participant in the first Course of Love group, one that was held as *ACOL* was being received.

that began to dismantle your ways of knowing. Metanoia is that chaos that is the loss of many of the old ways you once knew as being creative . . . to bring you to creation of The New. **Metanoia as a revolution recognizes what you have held back so as to bring forward who you truly are.**

The inner chaos you reveal "in" Metanoia, as you write Metanoia, "is" Metanoia—a revolution of its own. Revolutions are chaos. For you, chaos has been the experience of trying to share Metanoia even as its great disturbance is occurring in you.* Metanoia finds you at the juncture of your past and future, which is made up of your hopes and dreams and the qualities that express who you are.

You've been immersed in this great change. It is moving through you to close out the old and bring in The New: an astonishing knowing that will both confuse you and abide in you so that you yield to the awaited.

When Christie said of a new friendship: "He's got to let me keep suffering," you both knew that the feeling that causes you to feel chaos during "any transition" is amplified in grief, and part of the transition to The New is both grief and chaos.

Writing is your connection to your soul. Soul bonds are those that feel as though, if you were to be without them, you would not be you. You would not be complete. This is what we're sharing as we begin to put together this last book of our series. The bonds, the chaos, the losses, and the unfamiliar—all are disruptive as well as expansive energies.

---

* As *Metanoia* was being edited, I lost my only son, James Ian Mulvaney. See the end notes.

The unfamiliar "shared" knowing can be uncomfortable when it is first recognized and so, often, it is better left unrecognized until a maturing of the new knowing occurs.

Chaos

New knowing is chaos.

The word "chaos" is from the Greek. Its meaning is space: the formless matter that existed before the "ordered" and time-bound. Truly feeling the chaos of this change is the perfect experience to reveal Metanoia's revolution. It lets "your" time outside of time become "your" New. Metanoia returns you to "lack of order" to discover your needed freedom "from the old order"—the freedom that welcomes creation of The New.

"Here" it is all about re-cognition: returning to what was known before your adoption into the human race.

The realization then comes that no two humans know in the same way. Most take such comfort in feeling that they know in tandem with the collective, that they imprison themselves for no reason. True creativity will never imprison you.

The shared knowing that comes of creativity does not mean "the same knowing."

No two people know in the same way. But those who find comfort in feeling that they know in tandem with the collective, never seek release from this limited knowing.

Creative knowing is not limited. You can see this distinction easily with Michael because while you are creating together, you create from within different regions of the imagination. These regions are as distinct as Maine and Minnesota but are not separate. They are within you and between you, and you can take each other into different zones and partake of them. You might imagine this like regions of your brains lighting up in the same way at the same time, creating a shared orbit.

We each use our own metaphors to convey the meeting place of the imaginal . . . which can only be where you are . . . uniquely and individually. It's a paradox of everywhere and nowhere. It is nonexistent until two come together as one. In a sense it awaits your creation of it, and once you've created it, it awaits your knowing that this unity has simply been returned to you.

The two, come together as one, is the story of carrying new life in the womb of creation, but also the story of the birth, of the One becoming two—the duads of The New. Two as one creates new life in ways so diverse that no two thumb prints are the same. Few take in the wonder of this "fact" of human life. Yet "two" as one is also one as two in unity and relationship. Creativity is the same. Only the noncreative duplicate what was.

Creatives will be the forerunners of The New.

Mother, I am so "in another place" due to having joined with you and Jesus. I thank you "together" for bringing me your love and your words and this greater understanding of relationship between fellow creators. I wish to carry and to remain within this awareness of *union* as well as relationship. With great love and thankfulness I sense that this time has come forth so that creative and Holy Relationships find increase with each one's unique and shared embodiment of Soul. And, as part of that, I'd like to give thanks for Mike DiConti, who is new to the Center* since *Memoria* was

---

* The Center for A Course of Love is a non-profit organization whose initial purpose, to spread the message of *A Course of Love*, has been expanded to include support for the Way of Mary series as well.

published. He fills the space of treasurer with financial acumen and a fine sense of passion for *A Course of Love*.

The Open Door of Hope

I'm here in the cabin before five for the first time in about a week. The ground is black, the sky blueish . . . steely blue, with a line of light running through it about midway up the tree line.

As I watch for the sun's rising, I recall, as I so often do, words spoken by Fr. Adrian, words that speak of hope, not as a desire but as "a conviction, and a completion of what we're engaged in." I believe it is a good description of hope, a new and unusual description that is perfect for this time.

What happens on those days when I feel that Fr. Adrian knows me, is that he touches a knowing within me that rises, so that there is knowing and being known. That's what happens with the "holy ones" when they are "on"—whether they're writing or speaking, whether it's one-on-one or not. There's a *feeling* of knowing and being known that goes beyond identification with the personal and is still absolutely personal, so that you know the person is talking universal truth but feel as though it's meant for your heart in a sort of private way. This may happen because it's taken so far in—or just has that ability to go really deep within you—to that center, a place where there is recognition of a blending form of unity. There are many ways of being in creative relationships. Their primary attribute is desire for union.

The absolute ultimate in human satisfaction and joy is the union rather than the separation—whether it is human to God, or human to nature, or friend to friend. There's just no getting around it. It's the "blending" more so than the oneness that is the living thing within us . . . as if each little joining of parts is this lovely, lovely happening that is the essence of being alive.

When we're at work on joining the pieces of our psyche there might be frustration, but when we let go, and something clicks or falls into place, there is growth and movement and astonishment. Then we're ready for the next movement and the next . . . and each piece that gets connected is an increase of LIFE in the movement to wholeness.

Dialogue is one way that authentic people of good faith come together to give form to truth through heart and spirit, soul and voice. That's the beginning from which increase and fruitfulness springs. In dialogue, we gain our footing with a new way of being. The desire is not as much to "make things happen" as it is to make something *of what has happened already.*

When matters of interior significance occur, we can't ignore them, even if we try. We can't treat them as finite things, come and gone. There are always repercussions. The way we know is a rolling, ongoing event. It's not that it happens one day and, the next, becomes nothing more than a definition. That's the old way.

With Metanoia, we're out of the definition business. We've moved on.

Where Something Happens

I've lived the inner event that called me to *A Course of Love* for over twenty years—an event based on a dream that Mary Love shared with me of a "new Course in Miracles"—but only because *something happened*.

Mary and I began our spiritual explorations together, and I trusted that the dream was an announcement, a sacred event. I'd likewise had a dream in which I heard "you and Mary will have something to do with the end of ordinal time." From there, it was about fulfilling the call by bringing in what was meant to come, in the time it was meant to come.

The whole thing about a sacred event is that it sends out ripples that change *your* world, and then *the world*, even when you don't know it's happening. I've been further in the dark than I've realized. And it's okay. It's okay to start in the dark and follow our way to the light. We don't have to "know" to have new knowing affect us! The message is found *in its effect* rather than its meaning. You recognize a direction, an orientation . . . a way . . . a new way into the world. A new idea of the world, or of the Holy. It won't just remain in your head but will enter at the heart of your inner life and become manifest in the world through you. This happened to me in 2006 as I wrote *The Given Self*, so that I knew . . . "If you don't ever acknowledge that you've been called (or re-routed), there's never a significant change. If I hadn't acknowledged my reorientation, there'd be no *Course of Love*, then no solitude, no cabin, no dialogue, and no 'Christ to me'* experience."

I'm hung up on the mutual side of things. Mutual acknowledgment. Shared recognition. Reciprocal acceptance of a revealed experience. Collective re-routing. But my progression is firmly held in not knowing what I know until I know it. I've operated in the fog of unknowing many times . . . to rather miraculous ends.

It's one reason I ask my friends to be in Holy Relationship with me. It's like what happened between Christie and me almost two decades ago when we accepted that we were "in rebirth" together, the rebirth of a self of love called for in Chapter 14 of "The Dialogues." A few phone calls a week might not have seemed like any big deal but they were. We acknowledged being together in a transformation we couldn't direct.

The things that I "have" tried to direct never worked. Now, with Metanoia's turn around, I'm getting the "why" of it and understand that The New's own blended way is the coming of our revolution in consciousness.

---

* "I concluded that, from that point onward, each one would be Christ to me. The voice of the one heart and one mind was absolutely everywhere and in each living thing." *The Given Self*, p. 86

𝒯HE FIRST ACT: HOLY RELATIONSHIP

I call on Mother Mary to join me, just as some distinction, if not yet light, begins to find the ground along with me. This is our third book and we're familiar with each other's ways and our shared quest for movement from "the old" to The New.

In response to my call, Mary says, *Of course I will join you, even if you need no validation to proceed. Metanoia's revolution is a way to value life, your life, as well as all life.*

But you were freer then, in the days you speak of with Mary and Christie, and I want you to return to a sovereignty that is even greater now—to a freedom to be who you are and to join with others who are being who they are. This thoroughly counteracts the situations that have impaired you. Freedom is crucial and helps you with your manner of relating to all you have received.

The realization is ready to come that no one devalues life unless they devalue their own self. Ego is always a devaluation of the one it inhabits (not the opposite as so many believe).

I've noticed this devaluation of self in me too, Mary, and know that you've been working on it with me, and—through what we share—with all who have done the same.

This is the beauty of Holy Relationship. You have no ego with us, and you bring no ego to any Holy Relationship. **Holy Relationships are the end of ego and the beginning of genuine sharing.**

Yet, you did begin to devalue yourself long ago. This devaluation, along with your desire to be good, led to "anti-ego tendencies." Your Jesus then revealed to you that those tendencies were a real and present danger because you were not "called to selflessness but to

Self."* Any devaluation of self, as much as ego, limits your power. Ego and anti-ego are much the same. Either way, ego continues to live at the center of thought.

I admit that to devalue my life feels like destroying my life. Yet destroying my life hasn't always felt like a disaster. I've occasionally felt that I died to one life and resurrected to another. But really, it's only coming to mind now because of my great desire to continue to escape anything unnatural, like the "telling" I occasionally fall into.

That's a perfect way to put it. Everything is a dialogue now because of the great need to stop "telling." Here, we are letting readers be "in it" with us, and that is the design whose time has come. That's how the Holy Books were originally written, with stories occurring in the time of the prophets, the time of the saviors, and those following the lives of the Holy Ones. Many included a great deal of dialogue. And stories. Stories of times in which people lived, and their relationships with each other, with those in power, and with their God. Only parables were constructed with a moral at the heart of them. All else was spontaneous to the occurrences of what you call "life on the ground."

Like you, we had our concerns. We had hope, and we had heartache, even when we had holiness among us. It is the same with you. You innately look for this (hope and heartache) in current-time works, and for many years favored those of Thomas Merton, Thomas Moore, Parker Palmer, and others who shared "themselves"—their lives and feelings, along with the brilliant inquiries and insights they had to offer. These were "inner wisdom stories," even when faith waned, or self-criticism entered. This is what made them true stories, stories of the movement "to" this inner wisdom, gained by living. It is discounted

---

* ACOL D:1.9

at times, even with such luminaries as you've enjoyed reading. Scientific evidence, and an unquestionable and thus static knowing, (even when it's brief), is preferred over the variety of what is experienced. Interpretations of "holy works" sometimes only make it clear that people are no longer considered holy as they go about their daily trials and conversions.

Yet our people, like many in present time, moaned with the difficulties of their lives and with lives lost, and our God spoke to us, witnessed, and encouraged us. There is no lack, in other words, of precedent for bringing us your heartaches. And people do. People, individual people, continue to wail and be comforted. Prayers are still heard, even though the idea of it is considered quaint in many quarters.

The essential thing about such Holy Ones as history, mystery, and imagination find to be relevant, is that they have ways of making their presence known, and don't wait for you to be peaceful to come to you. All Holy Ones are in Holy Relationship with you, and with each one, my Mari. And it is your Holy Relationship, with Jesus and me, that naturally extends into this great desire to come together in a way that can only spread naturally, from you or anyone else.

This is what our revolution is going to inspire as we continue to extend Holy Relationship into the world.

When a Calling Finds You Endings Follow

While I was receiving *A Course of Love*, it was all I wanted to do. Feeling the same way about this dialogue with Mother Mary, I experienced another period of leaving "ought to" thoughts and actions behind. Our revolution is, in the main, not lofty. Who would look at the end of "oughts and shoulds" as a revolution? But these endings are part of our call.

Whatever is to come through Metanoia will be as choiceless as a love affair and will have as much to do with the one with whom you're sharing, as it does with what the engagement reveals to you. I say that only because I don't think the creation of The New that we are asked to take up would be possible otherwise. It's not that it's difficult . . . and yet it is. Focusing on one thing only is nearly unheard of. People who don't understand the commitment it takes, or that you might get divinely relieved of your ability to do anything else, may begin to worry for you.

And so it happened to me that, as I let go of all that I could reasonably let go, I thought of what it takes to be a creator, and how isolating it can be for some of us, and how essential it is, in this time, to give ourselves permission to "drop out" in order to "drop in" to something deeper than we've ever known before. We've been yearning so for it—for that depth. We desire so much to have our undivided attention requested and required. That's when we experience a call *and* a response.

Metanoia's revolution is really one of letting a new way of knowing inhabit us, or, to say it another way, letting a revolution in consciousness do what it does so we can accept where it takes us.

Somewhere between the acceptance of what I was called to "do" and also "be," I became confident that my time was being spent in the most essential way possible—in being a creator and finishing this written dialogue. But, at the same time, the "manner" of my difficulties told me something. They revealed that my life and this message are bound together.

Here's an example: One thing you can never do with work of this kind is force it. I knew I needed to listen "in" and abide by an idea of "right timing." All of my experience with these "received" books—what I did and what I ceased to do, the stoppages and the starting again—came of that kind of felt knowing, a knowing that is at the very heart of the new way.

That "new way" also stopped me from doing other things that were no longer mine to do, and the practical skills that fell away (many that I felt were still needed) have been, at times, a distressing counterpoint, but one that may speak to the same change. If we are to let the old fall away, maybe not having the skills to maneuver in an old way (uncomfortable as it can be) is actually part of entering and accepting The New.

It's not too mundane to desire a combination of feeling and knowing that suits "you." That's what will bring an end to your "oughts and shoulds." Even though I'm surprised all the time by what I encounter here, what I've experienced emerging in myself— (slowly . . . as you will see)—is confidence in my gift and my way, which has translated into this very power I've been talking about in our Way of the Marys series: the power to move out of "the old" and into The New.

We all have a sinewy vision of The New within us that needs to be both in-fleshed and fleshed-out. That vision comes of us. You and me. No two the same. It's a subtle but substantial power.

Along with Holy Mary, I would like to attract you to this movement to The New that Metanoia facilitates. The New will carry you to a sense of belonging in your life, in the changing time in which your life is unfolding, in your destiny to be a creator of The New, and in your heart's calling. It's the theme of this time in my life, as it may be in yours as well.

It will also turn you away from old and stagnant ways of knowing, as creation implies The New intrinsically. In whatever manner "you" create The New, it will come of what is "already your way," as writing (receptive and otherwise) is mine. I'm now convinced that being who we are each here to be, and doing what we are each here to do, is what will carry us into The New, and allow "eachness to replace thingness."*

---

* See *ACOL* C:20.39

Callings

A "calling" is a manner of experiencing as well as expressing who *you* are ... your fullest Self ... in the truest possible way. And that's the place from which each of us, and "we together," create The New. I hope to bring you, in a perfectly imperfect way, to a recognition and a "knowing" of *your* calling.

A Course of Love invites us with a call that's sounded in our hearts, and the "Dialogues" are about our response to being called. In them, Jesus asks, "How now will you respond to love?"

Gregg Levoy, in his book on callings, said, "A call is only a monologue. A return call, a response, creates a dialogue."[*] I love that quote and have often mentioned it when speaking of my call to *A Course of Love*. I knew *A Course of Love* was such a summons and have held it as my calling ever since.

But Mother Mary revealed even more, telling me, *"Once a work such as this begins, as with your* Course, *there is a cessation of the sense of being called and a feeling of being 'in it.'"*[†]

As soon as she said this, I knew it was true.

You and I, "we" are in relationship now. We are in it together. Togetherness doesn't end. "We are each other's own." The difference is we are not discrete but blended, and so the call now is to see the

---

[*] Levoy, Gregg. *Callings: Finding and Following an Authentic Life.* Three Rivers Press, 1997, p. 2.

[†] *Mirari*, p. 44 (paraphrased)

blending, the softening of form; a literal softening as what you see without the aid of perfect sight.

Mary tells me, *When you take off your glasses, as you often do when you're writing, what you see when you look out the window is clearly different than what you saw before you removed your glasses. It is the most perfect of examples, which is why we've spoken of this before.*

I understand, Mary. My work on "our" Way began to reframe my "resistance" to carrying on in an *old* way, into an "eagerness" to create in a *new* way.

That's the great turning of Metanoia, Mari. But the "new way" does not stand apart from anything.

I think it's helping me loosen my hold on *A Course of Love*. Maybe I stayed with "the calling" too long.

You give up nothing to move from "the call" to the "living of the call."

It really is different now, and I'm rather surprised I didn't see it sooner.

I had to develop a faith in The New before I could even begin to inhabit its spaciousness. I now see that I'm "there" in some manner that I've not gotten used to yet. And I like the idea of the blending. I even think I've experienced it. There aren't any defined boundaries anymore.

Yes! You and your brothers and sisters of the feminine are called to let go of your allegiance to the constrictions of the old. They limit you. Now you can embrace the expectant energy, readying to birth The New. This is your own vital life force—calling you to be a creator in your way. Creating anew is the way anything "new" comes into being.

I remembered Jesus saying, "Allow yourself to experience your arrival . . . your return to Self. Laugh. Cry. Shout or wail. Dance and sing. Spin a new web. The web of freedom."* I believe it came to mind because this liberating idea goes far beyond "allowing." What happens does not proceed by choosing but by feeling!

That is the best example you could give of Metanoia's turnaround.

Oh, thank you, my Mother. The idea of "being who we truly are" is the focus of everything coming to me "from" The New, "for" The New, and it's a momentous undertaking. When we're being true to ourselves, or I should say that, as "I've" made my way to "my truth," I found renewed commitment (if not yet energy) to be the creator I've always wanted to be. I'm so thankful, Mary. I suddenly see that there's no need to avail myself of anything that is "more of the same."

Yes, you're moving with Metanoia's difference in ways you haven't yet understood. That's what "this time" is about: Coming to be in receipt of what you know newly. This change from thinking and anticipating, to allowing the free flow of imagining and foreseeing, is a change that lets you catch up to your "new knowing," to be empowered by it, and to blend with it. To be it. To have no separation between knowing and being.

---

* *ACOL* D:Day9.2

THE PROPHETIC

And now, my Mari, it's time for you to know that you are of the prophetic tradition. Earlier I told you that you are of the way of the Word.* They go together.

I will help you attend to your understanding of what a prophet is very simply. A prophet is an announcer of The New. Sometimes the most obvious things are the last to be grasped.

Oh, Mary! Of course! How true that is. Yet despite all our talk of The New, I hadn't linked it with prophecy, even while it's the basic definition of being a prophet. Prophets announce The New!

This reminds me of how I was drawn to Abraham Heschel's book *The Prophets* two decades ago. I keep "going back" Mary, because I keep seeing the seeds that were planted in me long ago. For this "seed," which came before Amazon, I had to call around to find a copy and then drive to an antiquarian bookstore in Stillwater, Minnesota ("the first book town" in North America) to get an old hardcover volume. I loved it far more than I could ever have loved a new one. And it has a Philadelphia connection, too, as it was signed by Heschel for a Father McCreesh, and stamped with "Novices Library, Wernersville, PA." I suppose my desire to become acquainted with the prophets was my unseen acknowledgment of this new way. I've continued following those hints, clues, and subtleties all along . . . without knowing it.

Heschel's "Introduction" immediately inspired me. He wrote—and his words speak our language, Mary—of insight as "the

---

* *Memoria*, p. 341

beginning of perception to come: a break from our repetitiveness, requiring much intellectual dismantling!" This begins, he says, with "the cultivation of a feeling for the unfamiliar, unparalleled, incredible. It is in being involved with a phenomenon, being intimately engaged to it, courting it, as it were, that after much perplexity and embarrassment we come upon *insight* [emphasis added]—upon a way of seeing the phenomenon from within. Insight is accompanied by a sense of surprise. What has been closed is suddenly disclosed. It requires genuine perception, seeing anew."[*]

Mary, "intellectual dismantling" feels like what's happened in me!

Heschel says, in his way, what Jesus did in *ACIM*: "[T]o comprehend what phenomena are, it is important to suspend judgment."[†] And he suggests that "For the prophets to be alive and present to us . . . [we must] question prudence and impartiality,"[‡] He describes prophecy as "exegesis of existence from a divine perspective. To interpret prophecy from any other perspective— such as sociology or psychology—is like interpreting poetry from the perspective of the economic interests of the poet."[§]

How could I not love him!

It reminds me that I have said the words "suspend judgment" to myself many times since my early years with *A Course in Miracles*. It was one of my greatest takeaways. So it was a surprise to find, when I finally looked it up, that the phrase was only said once! Talking of the Holy Spirit, Jesus said:

---

[*] Heschel, Abraham. *The Prophets*. Harper & Rowe, 1962, p. xvi.

[†] Ibid, p. xvii

[‡] Ibid, p. xviii

[§] Ibid, p. xviii

[I]ts purpose is to suspend judgment *entirely*. Judgment always rests on the past, for past experience is the basis on which you judge. Judgment becomes impossible without the past, for without it you do not understand anything. You would make no attempt to judge because it would be quite apparent to you that you do not know what anything *means*. You are afraid of this because you believe that *without* the ego all would be chaos. Yet I assure you that without the ego all would be *love*.*

Suspending judgment, like prophecy, lets you see in a new way. As you already know, you aren't called to announce external events of the world, but to profess those inner events that much more truly change the world.

That's one of the reasons Jesus called us, in *A Course of Love*, to listen to our hearts:

Child of God, see you how important it is that you listen to your heart! Your heart does not want to see with judgment or with fear. It calls to you to accept forgiveness that you may give it and henceforth look upon the forgiven world with love.†

He also asks us to suspend disbelief,‡ which is basically saying, "Believe! Have faith!"

But it *is* a matter of *what* we believe in, isn't it? At the turn of the century, I returned to reading on the prophets with Walter Bruggemann's *The Prophetic Imagination*. He described the task of prophetic ministry as being "to nurture, nourish, and evoke a

---

* *ACIM Original Edition*, T15.45
† *ACOL* C:16.9
‡ *ACOL* D:11.12

consciousness and perception *alternative* to the consciousness and perception of the dominant culture around us . . . and to live in fervent anticipation of the newness that God has promised and will surely give."*

I'd like to think that's just what we're doing here, Mary, and what Jesus and I did with *A Course of Love*. That was my fight! To not have *ACOL* turned over to the dominant culture of my time—the "learning" culture.

---

* Bruggemann, Walter. *The Prophetic Imagination.* 2nd ed., Fortress Press, 2001, p. 3.

VULNERABILITY
AND THE MOVEMENTS IT INSPIRES

Dear Mary, I've also recalled a more contemporary example that spoke to me.

Twenty years ago, Brené Brown startled herself and the world with a bestseller on vulnerability. She spoke of this feeling, a feeling that so many of us wish we could abandon—in an entirely new way—as necessary. Her courage inspired me to share on vulnerability at my first major presentation[*] of *A Course of Love*. Maybe all of those who have been calling us back to feelings are the prophets of this time.

Brené Brown was quite surprised by her findings—findings that changed the direction of her life. This is the most common event that follows new knowing ... as you saw in your own life. With your call to work for God,[†] you not only left a job and friends you loved, but a literary agent. After years of writing you had gained an agent for your mystery novel, but you felt something so strongly about your new vocation that you canceled your contract. You didn't have to, but you did.

How seldom I've even thought of that. You'd think it would have haunted me, but it hasn't.

---

[*] Perron, Mari. "What's Going On." Miracles in the Mountain Conference, 2012, Cañon City, CO. Guest Presentation.

[†] Prior to my receiving of *A Course of Love*, while I was working at the University of Minnesota, I had a dream in which I was told "You can no longer sell your mind for money. Your mind now belongs to God." This dream played a profound part in the subsequent direction of my life.

This is one of the many ways you've acted on new knowing without realizing that you were doing so—which is the best (and nearly the only) way. You didn't think about "being sure," you simply knew what you needed to do at that time. **These are the new movements: movements based on what you "know" rather than what you think about what you know.** *This is called subconscious knowing and we invite all to look back on such instances of it in their lives.*

CREATIVE LIVES EXPRESS ANOTHER WAY

Other than *A Course in Miracles*, no single book affected my spiritual journey like Thomas Moore's *Care of the Soul*. It sparked my interest in cultivating, or maybe better said, appreciating the magnitude of the soul's gifts. At its end, Moore spoke of the World's soul and soul arts in a way that relates to our time in eternity. I find this long sentence to be a beautiful description of one of the lovely but ordinary ways I believe Metanoia arrives:

As we practice our daily arts, if only in the composing of a heart-felt letter, we are unearthing the eternal from within ordinary time, engaging in the special qualities, themes, and circumstances of the soul. Soul thrives as we jot down a thought in our diary or note a dream, and give body to a slight influx of eternity.*

The time we carve out for our "daily arts" comes of soulfulness, and soul always invites eternity. Eternity is where inspiration comes from, and it brings the holy realm to us whether we realize it or not. In that holy realm, solitude gives way to union "with." This is a place where you do not always want what comes, but you can't block the coming. Or better said, you await and welcome revelation until it arrives, and then are not so sure what you are committing to, for by merely beginning, you have already pledged yourself.

---

* Moore, Thomas. *Care of the Soul*. Harper Perennial, 1994, p. 304.

I knew this from having received *A Course of Love*. Such "reception" takes a heartfelt commitment. It's a promise. Once begun there's no turning back. You must fulfill the call.

And then you realize . . . it's what you always wanted . . . and how "The New arrives." The New calls us to discover and embrace what is ours to do. It seems to me we only give ourselves over when we know and feel that call. Great potential can be realized in this time if we only dare to let it come.

2014
ENCOUNTERS

I share this portion of an early visit from Mother Mary because she's speaking of the feelings we experience as we begin to make the great turning to The New.

M

These encounters (with altered states) weary you in much the same way as those encounters for which you cannot plan and for which you often feel you do not have the proper response. Yet you understand that this can't be explained. You can merely look to the nature of it for what it does to you, in your heart, mind, body, soul, cells. The desire to sleep. To rest. To stop. The desire to continue on. How many times have you sat with such feelings until your eyes began to close, heavy as anvils. "Tired" as you say, "for no reason." This has all been part of Metanoia.

This is the way it is, but momentary. A refreshment will come. This sort of tiredness need not make you feel weak, and it is important that you understand this now. You equate the tiredness of this "way of creation" with ordinary tiredness for no reason. This is "altered state" tiredness that will last for a while but eventually become something else, a different sort of altered state.

Don't be afraid to come now—not due to your weariness or for fear of not finding your own answers. Come for practice in this altered state with the belief that it will do the opposite with patience—it will increase your energy and your trust in yourself.

M

This was the last time Mother Mary visited me prior to the start of our Way of the Marys in 2018. The combined volume of *A Course of Love* had been published a few years earlier, in 2014, and I was engaged in a more public way with readers.

The Impossible Meets the Possible

The Return

"To the Call itself, time has no meaning."*

Daughter, I welcome you and all to this beginning of a revolution that opens you to a new way of knowing yourself—in the present, and in the whole of time—past and future yet unknown. Your soul's knowing expands in your new openness. By joining with the breadth of time, you find your soul as origin and originality, the source of the creativity and imagination that is your destiny in form.

As "your" revolution creates spaciousness "in you," it changes what you know and the way you know it without ever becoming immobile or static. You become creators of The New and prepare for a new movement in the heavens.

---

* *ACIM Original Edition*, M:1.2

Metanoia: The Great Turning

There is a difference in you and what you receive now because you composed a New Life as you created and published the first books of our Way of the Marys. We did that together then and are doing this together now. We are composing your New Life in dialogue and in actuality. We are a bit like two songwriters. I know the melody without which it wouldn't be a love song, yet it is only "together" that we find the heartfelt, the compassionate, the angry, and the prophetic words that reflect The New—The New of your time that will bring you and your sisters and brothers into new life.

There's a difference in our time together . . . one that is as real as your desire to be a writer . . . a desire that you feel is being tested. You have been reclaiming your life as your own and this is a powerful act to initiate. While you want to claim being a writer more than anything else, you realize that everything is different now. What you are affected by is the way time itself has changed. It has transformed itself and, in turn, transformed you.

You always had to "make time" . . . for you. It was an imperative of your nature as an introvert, a woman, and even a girl of depth. Your imagination was the most active part of your young years. You have invited me into "your" time, as I have invited you into mine. "Here" you compose yourself in your daily life. Here, nature is personified. Your alchemical self is immersed in an imaginal process of transformation and creation that accepts personification of everything (not unlike the way you did as a child)! The world is alive in you and for you. It is to these windows on the world that you bring your essential soulfulness. You bring it to us, your Holy Ones, along with your appreciation for finding us in the dark at the beginnings of your wonder-filled days.

There is, in A Course in Miracles, a phrase that says "Only eternity is real. Why not use the illusion of time constructively?"* The illusion has always been of time and ACIM conveyed this to you and sparked your readiness to receive A Course of Love and its insights on time. "Here" we've departed from the way of "using" time and raise our sight toward incarnation, as well as creation, in and of time. This, in itself, can let you see how immense the change of Metanoia is, because you no longer "use" and no longer learn. We change the meaning of illusion (to which so many cling) by revealing its location. The illusion only exists within the bounds of the constructed reality of the thinking mind. And we no longer construct.

Here we are deconstructing.

My Mari, everything is now about the turnaround of Metanoia.

---

* *ACIM Original Edition*, T:1.26

The Great Turning...in Time

You are in the midst of Metanoia's revolution. We have called it many things and you have worried over your lapses of memory because you are no longer "in time" in the way you used to be. Time "in you" has already been dismantled. You are an anchoress of The New in time outside of time. This is a blessing. It has taken you out of bounds of the old. Many are joining you, and what we speak of is for them as well as you, because you are not *who you are newly "in the old" concept of time, but* are *who you are newly in the time of The New. The Great Turning of Metanoia's revolution, for which you've been prepared, does the same for all who return to residing in spaciousness.*

In 2018 your prophetic sister, Rhetta Morgan, announced this turn to you and Mary Love. She saw it as the call of the ancient Essene midwives. While you didn't know in what way this day was prophetic, after returning home from that gathering in Philadelphia, you began to hear from me. And your soul sister, Mary Love, began hearing from Mary Magdalene. You felt that soulful connection then but hadn't seen the fullness of the announcement that I now share with you.

On that day in 2018, Rhetta and Helen sang of "The Great Turning."[*]

What is a revolution but a great turning? Metanoia is the great turning wherein "a new time of no time" awaits the return of love and Self.[†]

---

[*] See https://www.youtube.com/watch?v=OLICxt-wLuU. "In this great turning we will learn to lead in love."

[†] *ACOL* C:20.13

I think I get it, Mary. Oneness prevails because of eachness! "Eachness replaces thingness."* I've always thought there was a whole new theology in that amazing Chapter Twenty of *A Course of Love*.

Receiving "The Embrace," you were out of bounds of the constructed reality, and were being introduced, through that great turning, to Metanoia and the imaginal, both. Metanoia turns you away from your habits of mind, putting you within the soul's domain and opening the possibility that is the imaginal gift.

'Thingness' is over, and your identity no longer stands in form but flows from life itself. Your beauty is the gathering of the atoms, the order in chaos, the silence in solitude, the grace of the cosmos. Our heart is the light of the world.†

We are one heart. We are one mind. One creative force gathering the atoms, establishing the order, blessing the silence, gracing the cosmos, manifesting the light of the heart. Here we live as one body, experiencing communion, the soul's delight, rather than otherness. It is a seamless world, a tapestry where each thread is vibrant and strong. A canticle where each tone is pure and indivisible.‡

From here your life becomes imaginal.§

What but Christ's vision would I use today when it can offer me a day in which I see a world so like to Heaven that an ancient memory

---

* *ACOL* C:20.39
† *ACOL* C:20.4
‡ *ACOL* C:20.4-6
§ *ACOL* C:20.10

returns to me? Today I can forget the world I made. Today I can go past all fear and be restored to love and holiness and peace. Today I am redeemed and born anew into a world of mercy and of care; loving kindness and the peace of God.*

---

* *ACIM Original Edition*, W2:306.1

The Dim

"Dim" might be a good word for this time, time caught between day and night, between the sleeping and the waking, between the eternal and the transient. The quiet mind and the active wonder. It's restful, this in between time that Mother Mary and I speak of.

The in between is not a lesser place to be.

One day soon I'd like to start at sunset and write until sunrise, just to feel it. To once again be writing just to write. Then I'm at my best.

The "book" forms when I'm done writing. When I'm "working on a book," something else creeps in. I leave all of that behind... "here" ... in the dim. In the dim of the in between, when I am with me, I am with you.

If you find yourself moseying along with me, that will be the best way. You will see for yourself.

SOUL

It is eleven o'clock for me and six for Coralie* in Spain. We are looking at each other and hearing one another's voices on our computers. When we are wrapping up, she says, "I want to read something to you." And then there it is: the surprise, the beauty—the stunning beauty of hearing your words spoken, Mary. It takes me a minute to realize they are ours. And I put my hand over my heart.

Your soul knows you. Your soul knows "for" you. Your soul goes before you, showing you the way. The soul carries to you an image of your life to which you spend your life responding.†

And so, sometime after the dark of evening was falling, on another call, Lee‡ said much the same thing about the beauty of the words, and I again got such a catch in my heart, and even thinking of it now, it comes, and the tears which only hinted on the call, well up and sting. I grope for Kleenex in the dark and am so glad that I know, by heart, where everything is.

---

* Coralie Pearson, friend and translator of *ACOL* Spanish Edition

† *Mirari*, p. 201

‡ Lee Flynn, a dear friend and *ACIM* scholar

Light and Soul

Mary, I hope I am to be in reverie of every single day, every bit of life, every season. I look out and it is like the time before the naming of things. The world is empty of thingness, pristine and new.

I welcome the world to the second coming along with me. We are in it together.

There is a ray of light on the horizon—small, straight and sure. I move my body this way and that, and it remains. It is a luminous form I've never seen before. It is horizontal, clear, brilliant and steady.

The line of light is here. The lineage of light.

This is real.

I have a sense of enormity running through my body, and the familiar fullness in my womb. The light before me is white, like a reflection. I move again to be sure it's not coming from elsewhere.

I wish I knew what time this began. It's 7:22 now.

When day comes, this kind of light would usually disappear, but the sky has blued now, and it's not diminished. It arose in the early black darkness, and it remains in this coming of day.

Before my eyes, the deep blue of eight o'clock reveals clouds on the horizon, but none mar my vision of the line of light.

I think of recent weeks when I sat with the manger, and how the cabin has felt like my manger.

Then... Jesus, Mary, and Joseph! I see it! The direct line from you! The line that is of The New birthing! For all that is sacred, The New is birthing and holy-ing the world.

And the light is still here.

I hear from within: "Know in your heart that none of the things you can define are essential. None of the ways that you believe they come are the entire breadth and truth of them. What is not the entire truth is simply partial. There is no condemnation, no trivialization, even of things. There is only the life-giving and that which removes life. Life is never destroyed, only disconnected from its own awareness of living." I know this is my soul talking.

In this time, Mary says, *it is important for you to hear the voice of soul rise into words, as you are of the way of the Word.*

In the world's future it won't matter what this is called. Call it the muse, inspiration, the flow, the fire, the idea, the revelation, the beautiful brain, or the robust heart. Or call it life. With reverence for every life. Every life.

Anima Mundi: The World Soul

The world, too, has soul.

The orientation of your soul is toward bringing time and space together in you, which is, in effect, an acclimation to the soul of the world. This togetherness coincides with the birth and creation of a new duad in your destiny field "where you will meet those who, along with you, create the space for all choices of love . . . and none other than choices of love."* Here, duads are formed by those who, in spaciousness, know they are no longer separate. This change takes place in the deepest and furthest reaches of your being.

Here, I refer to the Greek anima mundi *to speak of a world ensouled. The Greek meaning of* μετάνοια *is often spoken of as changing one's mind. But this is a change that only comes from a transformative change of heart (a part too frequently left out of its meaning). With Metanoia, you become one who naturally sees the heart of the world beating all about you, as well as within you. The within comes to be in union with the spacious totality, where there is nothing that is* not *part of you. Your revolution in consciousness grants you the sight by which you find soul "without" as you see all from the view of the soul "within." The within and without become one in spaciousness.*

Now you make the major leap in consciousness that is the result of thoroughly taking in all that is with sympathetic understanding. By combining your expanded sense perception with an understanding heart, you know that there is nothing that is not "naturally" imbued

---

* *Mirari*, p. 99.

with soul. You see that your soul's view of life is already changing "you." Now—together in union—you greet your desire to embrace eternity and bring to wholeness all that has been separated "in time" and "by time."

With your ensoulment of "your world," all realms beat to the same pulse, the same heartbeat. The rhythm of your acclimated heart brings constancy and completion to your soul. And, as your heart rocks you, your soul begins to correspond to the heartbeat of "your" world which, through your extension, is identical with "The World." This is creation. This extension becomes tantamount to Anima Mundi as the vital force of the world.

"We are the heartbeat of the world. This is creation. This is God. This is our home."[*]

You rock, my Mari, from this extension, and are rocked from within this embrace.[†]

As "you" continue your release of time, you catch up to what you know, and move on from the childhood of this consciousness that has adhered to time alone. It is the imposed measure of time, and the relentless neutrality and universality teaching calls for, that together have deadened your ability to see time's own creative nature, even while it still responds, season to season with its own wonders.

But now, as we awaken time outside of time—in time—many will yearn to adjust to our "anything but neutral," "anything but separate" reality. Resurrecting soul is what propels recognition (re-knowing) of an ensouled world and your incarnation within it.

---

[*] ACOL C:20.10-11

[†] Since beginning this work I have begun to rock unconsciously and rather continuously, as if in a rocking chair.

The turn we have taken, with Metanoia's revolution, is the dis-remembering of what was "known" and the recollecting of what has been obscured. What has been obscured in the past is revealed again in this great turning of what we are calling "The New." We call it that because it is new to you, but also because The New is not static and does not stop becoming New.

The New is the return of the love and soul that create The New endlessly, without dismissing the felt wisdom of the Earth, sky, water, space, the feminine and masculine of humanity, or divinity. Here, in this turnaround, this knowing again, the assurance comes that feelings are indispensable in saving the soul of the world. Anima Mundi.

Jesus was always welcoming those who could come to new life through great desire for life to be new. This desire sparks Metanoia's expansive change of heart. We are turning away from many old ideas by simply looking toward The New with vision and with intense desire to participate in the new way of creation.

Here we move beyond regret, revealing Metanoia as the change in which each one feels reunited in the embrace of God's love.

In this great turning we live in Love, and in that way, let Love lead.

Wonderings:
In and Within the Dark

Oh, Mary. I so thoroughly feel the world's soul "here." I don't know how to share the physical part of the feeling I have as I "enter" the dark of the cabin and the woods, but I'd like to try. I call it being "in and within," and I use the same expression for my experience of your Holy Words. I am in and within those words through the relationship they create with me as they arrive.

It's like the feeling of coming home to a surrounding presence of love, or the way you feel on those days in which you are one with the life you're living, or when you're returning from somewhere "else" to the intimacy of yourself. Your home has come into being within you as well as being a presence that holds you, a structure in which you abide.

"In and within." Being *in and within* the dark, another meaning is implied—that of awareness on both sides, sides akin to inner and outer but not quite that.

This is how it is with me and the dark, particularly that of early morning. I become part of it. I "feel" part of it and can respond from its depth! I am less contained and less distinct. Strangely, at the same time, being "in" the dark I have, I suppose, an "embracing" experience, even an experience of "the embrace." I'm held in it, by it. In those first "readied moments" of sitting in its surrounding presence, I am attended. The dark leans in, inclining toward me. Physical sensations of "depth," like deep space, arise as from a lingering presence, held like the sunrise until the exact right moment. Mystery looms and I respond to the power of open space with my own open space.

"Here" the depth "in me" greets the depth of dark like it's coming home. I feel the void from which everything first arose, and it rises again in me, or draws me deeper into it. It's mutual, a mutual draw, an agreement between me and the life of the day. I enter at the beginning . . . to where I don't "know" what will be and yet am in touch with knowing.

And there's this whole sense of this being the natural cycle—to draw out of the dark the knowing that corresponds to and has that need for sleep and dreams. Sleep and dreams and experiences of the dark arise from our wakefulness to a time zone other than the one in which we gather our wits. Instead, we are being in and within our own experience—our own natural cycles, our own dreams, and our own depth. We have stepped out of time and into eternity.

Mari, you have just described the qualities of Metanoia.

Oh Mary, that would be so wonderful.

𝒯HE GIRL IN THE VELCRO DRESS

On my birthday I awoke to the words, "Time heals all wounds."

Before I left my bedroom, and uncommonly for me, I was looking out the window and imagining that, if time had a face, it was there. I pondered how the moon was still present somewhere, but hidden. I saw how, while the clouds were visible, they were impermanent. Then I felt the sky as the blanket over the bed by which I knelt. The sky, I thought, was of my aspirations. The earth, my ruminations.

My friend Christina Strutt had sent me a web post, "The Girl in the Velcro* Dress,"† at just the right time. It had affected her and now it affected me.

Knowing how much I liked it, Christina wondered if I wanted to talk. I said I had a problem on my mind and was trying to feel into how I wanted to deal with it, but when no new ideas were forthcoming, I made the call. It soon became obvious that I didn't need to say or do anything. The problem wasn't mine. The allegory of the self-fastening dress made this clear.

---

* VELCRO® is the brand name for a specific manufacturer's hook and loop fastening system. The title of the web posting has been retained from the original for accuracy, but use of the word "Velcro" as a noun or adjective violates the manufacturer's trademark guidelines.

† Plett, Heather. "The Girl in the Velcro Dress: An allegory for those who carry too much." *Heather Plett,* 11 Feb. 2020, https://heatherplett.com/2020/02/girl-velcro-dress-allegory-carry-much/#:~:text=much%20%2D%20Heather%20Plett-,The%20Girl%20in%20the%20Velcro%20Dress%3A%20An%20allegory.those%20who%20carry%20too%20much&text=Once%20there%20was%20a%20girl,mother%20and%20grandmothers%20before%20her. Accessed 18 Feb. 2020.

In the story, the narrator is a girl who had, herself, made the self-fastening dress, "stitching it together out of all of the bits that had been passed down to her by her mother and grandmothers before her. Into the stiches were woven the messages and beliefs from her culture, her religion, her family system, the media, and the grown-ups who knew no better because they wore [self-fastening] clothing too." She also carried the expectations and needs others wanted her to meet, as these could easily be attached to her dress. In the story, the dress became heavier and heavier until the girl, now a woman, could no longer carry its weight. Eventually, she realized she could let that weight go, and in the process, begin anew.

The power of this allegory snuck up on me like a whisper, another among many telling me that I was done with an old part of my life. In my dialogue with Christina, we both felt it . . . a completion. The New had come. The old was over. We were done. We'd *been* done. We just hadn't seen it. And peace descended.

These rare times feel powered from elsewhere in a way that I see as being of The New. I saw us as its dynamic and vivifying forces— us as the spontaneous clarifiers of some human to human, or perhaps soul to soul, bond. Animated, and with enough sounding, we drown everything else out, not in volume but in incitement to speak, to see deeply, to howl. And then we transcend something that's been holding us back and discover that which cannot be forgotten. We can no longer return to a time when we didn't know it could be this way. Such grace came to us as conviction. I haven't yet taken in the full measure of my soul or her way of communicating, but I have my precious "soul" people who I won't let go without a fight and won't summon too often to be a pest. And I see I can be content with little because it is so much.

Suddenly then, after a quiet evening, I saw it has always been enough. Real connection is still what takes me away from what I'm leaving behind. A few good people can do that. Even a mission, and even my great desire to be with you, Holy Mary, and Jesus, have never lessened my desire for meaningful personal sharing where something "true" actually occurs. When two become as one we're always met by something greater. It's an almost impossible thing to express, but after once having experienced "the truly real," person to person, you are ruined for the polite, the insincere, the artificial . . .

You can't go back.

And then, I, who still vacillated at times between this and that, took up the choiceless path "again." Here, I get to "stay with the real." I imagine my yen for solitude was sparked partially by feeling it was better to be alone than to meet and not be allowed access to another's heart, and to find that the other had no desire to know mine. What I wanted seemed to defy the rules of social engagement.

And I finally saw that it may be just the right time to defy those rules.

Then the words, "Hear me now," entered my mind. I felt that having transcended this communication "problem," I had closed some kind of gap.

Hear me now. It would never, my Mari . . . A Course of Love *would never have been what it is without you, just as* A Course in Miracles *would not have been what it is without Helen. Neither would be the same if they'd had a different scribe. That's what you've been trying to say all along in what you call your complaints, isn't it?*

This was so far from my mind (or I thought it was) that I'm surprised by her words. I feel shocked and tell her so. "What impact,

Holy Mary. Thank you," I say, relieved that it's been said in such a simple and perfect manner that even I can accept it. "Yes. Thank you with all my heart, Mary."

Before these words were spoken, I didn't realize such a sentiment could reach in and tap my full to bursting heart. If I were literally speaking to you right now, you would hear the gush of tears in my voice and see them in my eyes. Finally, I am understood. Being understood, I finally understand myself!

And, you are literally speaking to me right now, and I do know you. With this desire met, you can finally move on, can't you, dear one?

Yes! You have given me the right words. How silly it feels to never have been able to come up with them myself. Jesus' book, written with anyone else, would not be the *Course of Love* that is here and that will outlast me and my kids, and that may touch generations to come. Talk of a great desire waiting to be met! How long I will be feeling this relief! Forever long. And in how short a breath will I be able to move on to newly blessed desires, of which, my Mary, this is one. And you have just redeemed me within it. I couldn't be more grateful.

On this day we have closed out the old and opened The New.

And I am made new on my 65th birthday.

2020

A TIME OF TRANSFORMATION

Mirari was completed in mid-2019 and published in December of 2020. My reception of *Memoria* followed on the heels of *Mirari*, and was begun *and* completed, aside from the end notes, in 2019 as well, but awaited editing. It was published in early 2022. *Metanoia* began in the midst of this time. Selections from relevant journal writings that relate to the many changes that were going on as the three books began to come together are included in this section.

The Start of the Pandemic

March 13, 2020

A beautiful sky of clouds before the moon, all in movement. White fluffs, blue darkness, invisible wind. It's 5:18, and I've been here a bit after waking before 4:00.

The coronavirus that began at the start of this year is expanding and yesterday's paper put two recognizable names to it: Tom Hanks and his wife Rita Wilson, about the sweetest acting couple ever. An editorial that spoke of the flu epidemic after WWI gave context to what now seems unprecedented. They're talking of having classes online and halting sports events. Travel is being banned all over.

I wonder how Mia* is doing in her waitressing job, and Angie and Henry at the school. Ian reported to Donny that stores were out of toilet paper and paper towels. People are stocking up—already—and there are only five cases of the virus in Minnesota.

How do you know, at the start of anything, what will come to be? I pray for all the world and imagine all our bodies being spared painful deaths, and that parents and grandparents will not bury their children or grandchildren.

I imagine a blessing where the world slows down, more people stay home, and the streets are quieter. The pace is slower. Sheets hang on clothes lines and the scent of clean air clings to them.

---

* Mia and Angie are my daughters. Ian is my son, and Henry is my grandson.

This morning's sky reminds me of the immense, downy, morning clouds of childhood. Even though it's only 5:34 and light hasn't come, the look is of day, and so a beautiful blending.

I am in love, elated by morning. At 6:20, the sky is still satiated with crisp winter air, the clearest, purest looking blue, even though it's dark. The clouds line up, one after another, an infinity of clouds, moving, moving, moving, and the moon is keeping an eye out on the world. I know you are too, my Holy Ones.

You are each the perfect ones to invite the realm of the Holy of Holies into your hearts.

March 14, 2020

The paper has announced a dispensation from church attendance for Catholics, due to Covid-19.

I'm thinking of how the internet has become the thing that connects people, and how we can get together, and conferences can even occur without anyone needing to leave home. People are being "forced" away from the crowd, and they find ways to gather even so. No matter how short or long-term this pandemic may be, it has already changed things. Everything moves us along in some fashion, toward the fulfilment of our destiny, individually and as a people created to live and love freely. And what appreciation we'll gain.

The sky is lightening into gray and is still full only of itself with no distractions. I blessedly mimic my friend Sky for this brief time.

Then a flash of unknown origin arrives, a light I can't describe, low over the fence—something I've never seen before. A "blob." It's near oval in shape but not precise, more like a child's drawing of an oval. It makes me feel visited and gives me a Mirari moment, a moment of wonder followed by my "wondering"—only it's the type of curiosity that doesn't expect an answer about what it means or what it "was," but instead asks what it heralds. Isn't that part of our Way of Mary? To wonder what is being heralded, what is being announced?

And then I look up, and the sky is flaming pink!

Now the vision of the women and the wild dogs feels nearer than before. The women around the campfire. And whatever elder status, wisdom, fearlessness there is to be had.

The Wound of the Womb

March 18, 2020

A light flickers across the top of the fence. It might as well be a falling star, so much is any omen of presence welcome. I realize how true it is that I don't often feel the impact of things until I write. The new virus has become a pandemic and I'm thinking about this when a sensation arises suddenly, of the "virtual" having come into existence for a reason, to serve a greater purpose in our isolation. I wonder about that word—virtual—and turn on the light to look it up. Basically, it is "in effect not in fact." But the word "effect" is about something that comes into being! What is more real? A "fact" is supposed to mean "a truth," but does it? I haven't been sure with the politics and biases that are dividing us, but maybe the quality of news will change with the virus.

So far it is still dark in the woods: ebony trees, dim shadows, mysterious sky, and without my glasses on, all else is composed of shapes not yet fully formed. My feelings concerning the virus and the changes that have ensued hadn't taken form either until today. Now they have—in sorrow for the loss of life, and in a personal fear, of life as I know it going away. This is very nerve wracking in a way I can't say.

There is always a moment, one moment in one particular hour of one particular day, when a dawning new reality comes forward and you shudder under the view of the images it carries. A time of repatterning the world is upon you at 6:44 AM on this 18th day of March, 2020.

You drew an image of the virus yesterday. Why? You didn't know.

Also, you began to uncover some of your biggest fears, and I do mean fears. It began with your daughter's hysterical laughter. Look up the word hysterical, my Mari.

Hysterical: A condition variously characterized by emotional excitability, excessive anxiety, sensory and motor disturbances.

Hysteric: suffering in the womb(!) (from the ancient notion that women were hysterical more often than men).

Hysterectomy: a removal of all or part of the universe (I typed universe! I meant uterus, which is another word for womb).

The wound of the womb.

Oh, Mary... my mother's mother, my southern grandmother,[*] was committed to this horrid place where they forced a hysterectomy on her. The Central State Hospital[†] in Milledgeville, Georgia was the largest mental hospital in the world at the time—and one of the most notorious.

Oh, my Lord and Mother.

The wound of "the womb of time" is what is being corrected, in multitudinous ways, in this century of the women.

Can you see this "crisis" of change in the physical, as a herald of change? A change in which what needs to happen is imminent. When

---

[*] Ivie Jones Diprima

[†] The hospital, which was founded as the Georgia State Lunatic, Idiot, and Epileptic Asylum, has been in continuous operation since 1842. Media attention in the late 1950's called attention to the squalid conditions and inhumane treatments to which the patients were subjected.

what needs to happen is going to happen? When Metanoia's revolution must become apparent?

I hadn't thought of it that way, and I'm not sure it's occurring.

What, my Mari, is the basic "remedy" to the threat of this time? This pandemic?

Isolation.

Yes. It is a move from constant contact to refraining from interaction with the group and the masses. Recall the word "solo." Solo is the root of the Hebrew shalomo. Shalom . . . peace. So many fear being alone. When it comes to the physical almost everyone fears they'd not have the skills to survive. Survival needs were the beginning of all banding together. What will isolation reveal to individuals, groups, and countries? What could bring about more change? More . . . unification? Unification without enmeshment? Unification without eradication of differences?

Metanoia commences to invite radical unification . . . within each one. It is wearing the inside . . . out. Two in one and one in two.

The New will not be as positioned with the seed and the root as with the water and the womb. Water can move through gaps and fissures; water smooths and flows to equilibrium.

What is more necessary than a balance of opposing forces, none more primal than the masculine and feminine? Equilibrium is what keeps you positioned properly in your orbit so The New *can find* You. Each One. Each One *specifically. This symmetry is what is occurring now within time and within you. It is disintegrating the old and forming The New in equal measure. In equal measure. At the same "time," my daughter.*

It reminds me of a passage from The Dialogues:

This is a time of convergence, intersection, and pass-through of the finite and the infinite, of time and no time. Time has not yet ceased to be, but as you are in a state of transformation, so too is it. Again I remind you, *as within, so without*. As you let go of time's hold on you, it will let go of you. Time will seem to expand but will actually be contracting into nothingness. **Time is replaced by presence,** by your ability to exist in the here and now in acceptance and without fear.*

I, and all of my closest friends, are experiencing this, and I find it comforting **that it's not just me**.

And you can see that at the same time that all is collapsing, all is being reformed. This, too, is the inside/out, outside/in revolution of Metanoia, ending the division and denial of what gives life, what takes life away, and the connection between them. This is as much a part of this revolution of consciousness as is honoring the feminine.

But here, you and many women, including your Grandmother Ivie, and all the women descended from her, and each one born with a need of the healing of the wound of the womb, will be consoled. In this healing we include time herself—time that gives birth to the day you now see.

We include many women and men who have experienced fetal trauma in the womb during pregnancy, including your Angela. We include those pregnant women and the babe(s) they aborted, the men who walked away and the men who helped make these decisions, whether in support of the mother's choice, or not. This is a very sensitive subject, I know, and one you are not eager to express, but do so we must . . . to end suffering.

---

* *ACOL* D:Day7.7

Do you realize, my daughter, that this is ours to do? **We are here to end the suffering of the womb, including the womb of time.** *When Rhetta saw you in the lineage of the Essene midwives, she was indeed prophetic. The wounds of the Grandmothers, the Mothers, and the Daughters have been awaiting this rectifying time. I speak of this without any judgement, with no reference to anything but healing.*

As I expressed in Mirari, *Mary Magdalene was not one to "leave any wound untended. Her strength came from having been honed by pain." And "her strength was exquisite tenderness." I assured you that "You could see Jesus gathered with the twelve and going to death alone, as the time that is passing, and the Marys joined together to tenderly release the life that was, to the life that will be . . . as the way of The New."**

This we do, together as one, to heal the wounds of the womb and of time . . . for they go together. Life "in" time is life "given" unto time through "birth into time." But here we are creating a new time. A spacious time of re-creation. Our explorations of the human heart are generating a newly spacious habitat.

We are the heartbeat of the world.

The Hush of Love is that from which the world arose into sound and light. This was not the creation of the pregnant or the gestation of the babe in the womb surrounded by the heartbeat, the rush of blood through veins, the gastronomy of the body. Love in its conception was, and is, All. All that would arise out of the great silence.†

---

* *Mirari*, p. 206

† *Ibid.*, p. 85

All that arose out of the great silence, in perfection and innocence, will return or be healed in Metanoia's Great Turning.

What will arise, may be both actual and metaphorical, personal and universal. For when "your" orbit turns, as a whole, to its original creation, the universe has turned as well. With each fraction of a turn, new life makes its first sounds, soundings that echo out to embrace all.

LET YOURSELF FEEL LOVED

March 22, 2020

Each date feels more important than the last, strangely significant, even when there's no association. Because they're of time, dates have import too.

It's Sunday. The first in my life in which there are no masses said with people in pews. Not anywhere in the United States.

And it's still noisy. I don't get it. Unless the busiest people in the world are truck drivers delivering goods. And if no one is going to work but them, how long will there be "goods"?

California, New York, Chicago, San Francisco—they're all on lock down. The whole world, just about, is "grounded." Isn't that interesting...

March 23, 2020

I'm in tears my Mary, thinking of precious lives being lost, feeling certain lives like memories, even with your message of hope.

Picked up my Joyce Carol Oates' book* and opened to her expression of grief over one life, that of her editor, Henry Robbins. She writes how she wanted him as a friend "at a near distance." I love that. She describes how she remembers him: his expression,

---

* Oates, Joyce Carol. *The Journal of Joyce Carol Oates 1973 – 1982*, edited by Greg Johnson, Eco, 1988.

his clothing, his words, his gentleness. And I think again of my editor friend Steve Lehmann who faded out of my life. I "see" scenes with him. Scenes that remain in my view. Here in the house at the dining room table where we edited *Peace*.* Another in the beautiful garden deck of a restaurant overlooking Grand Avenue where we met for a final review of the first publication of *The Dialogues*. In the backyard, walking to the woods (before the cabin was built) in the full lushness of summer, and him likening the grapevines between the yard and woods to the cornfield in the movie *Field of Dreams*.

My God, it's hard to not have closure on that one. It's hard when people fade out of your life. And there seems to be a bigger fade going on than ever before. There are many ways to lose people. But I pray this healing time extends to this predicament we're in.

It's 6:20 with a new snow having fallen, just a dusting but a sticky one, soft and lovely, the kind where I leave footprints that are clear impressions. And it's hard to settle in, my Holy Ones. I'm dangling here, in this time of getting *Memoria* ready, with too many words and no words. And a tender heart after such a sweet exchange with Lee yesterday, sweet mainly because he doesn't make things into what they're not.

Now there's an expression. There's a good way to be. Because there are lots of people who do make things into what they're not. That's when the confusion sets in.

It's so cold. I watch as a bunny tries to get moving and can't. She flattens her ears over the top of her head. The poor dear. We're all a bunch of poor dears wishing our mothers were around to take care of us again.

---

* *Peace* is Book 3 of The Grace Trilogy.

Just relax. I'm here for you and for all. Let yourself feel loved. LET YOURSELF REST.

March 24, 2020

6:11 in a deep, deep dark. I don't know when I've seen it so dark as this. I'd bet there's a light out somewhere. If so, I'm glad of it.

Donny and I both spoke yesterday of wanting to go to the eye doctor. As soon as you can't go, or feel reluctant to go, you feel foolish for not having gone when it was the easiest of choices.

But then again—it wasn't. There's been something going on for a while, and I feel like it may have traveled across borders more than the virus. An inner, underlying desire to stop it all, the constant maintenance of the body as much as the busy interfering of the social and work-related pestering! Yes, it's all been pestering us, and when you didn't know it, you didn't care, but when suddenly you know? Then it becomes more than mere annoyance. You begin to see why people go off the grid . . . to a place where they feel they can't be found, where they can break free.

Breaking Free is the End of Learning

What could be a bigger revolution in consciousness than the end of learning?

Mary, sometimes, I feel like our knowing comes in unison. Usually, I come to know your words as you speak your words. But sometimes, as soon as you begin to speak, I know I was ready for, or had a precognition of, exactly what you would tell me.

It's been said, more than a few times within this work, that I don't yet "know what I know," the implication being that I know far more than I think I do. I feel that this is true. I "know" this is the truth and the bane of many—women particularly—each for our own reasons.

For me it has been the crux of my love affair with this work for twenty years: finding the way that I know innately. It happens with anything that causes me to understand what I've felt, or to feel that I, myself, have been "gotten," understood, accepted, made part of something, or that I have made something "real or true" a part of me. All of it has had "speaking and being heard" at the heart of it.

Speaking and being heard.

I begin to wonder: what's stopping us from speaking and being heard? Listening to my friends—and hearing them—helps me know what "I" know. They spark me to my own knowing, and I can imagine that the same occurs for them when they hear me. Acceptance (our own) that we "know together," goes along with "knowing and being known." It makes all the difference because with acceptance you can admit how you feel and, from how you feel, how you know.

It's part of the unlearning we're asked to do in *A Course of Love:*

[Y]ou must be able to look at and see reality for what it is. Just as we are telling you that new beliefs and ideas will lead to a new reality, old beliefs and ideas led to the old reality, a reality that will still exist for some even after it changes completely for you.

This will seem even more inconsistent with a benevolent universe than it once did because of the difference between one reality and the other, a difference that couldn't be seen until it was represented in an observable manner, something you will now do.

You would think that this disparity would be divisive and extremely uncomfortable and even rage-producing for those still living in illusion. But it will be much more tempting to be divisive, uncomfortable and rage-producing for those living in the New.

This is unlearning taking place. It may feel frustrating and be tinged with anxiety, anger, confusion, perplexity, even rage. You will doubt that these are the proper feelings of a person living love. Yet they are common feelings of unlearning, and should be accepted as such.[*]

"Learning" is really gone now, isn't it? At least for those of us who have gotten this far... whether we understand it or not.

Do you even need to ask? You said it yourself. What could be a bigger revolution in consciousness than the end of learning? With unlearning, despite its frustrations, you realize that "you already are" experiencing the onset of a new way of coming to know.

---

[*] *ACOL* D:Day25.13-19

Easter Sunday, April 12, 2020

This that I do is obsession, like the way the wind feels when it batters-up and begins to fulfill its prophecy.

DAILY REVERIE

August 28, 2020

Friday, during a thunderstorm. 5:33 and the first time, I think, that I've ever come out to the cabin without my glasses. The thunder shakes me where I sit, a vibration that feels as if it comes up from the floor, starting off the morning right away with the mystery of earth and sky and their lack of separation. It is really very glorious and just a little scary. I left my umbrella inside for fear of the lightning. My little moth is acting like she's going crazy. She flew right onto my face, like kissing my cheek.

August 29, 2020

This morning I stood in the dining room with my papers again, and again felt like an insane person who will not possibly make it through this editing.* I MUST be done. At this point, I do not even know if I can do it, or how to do it.

    Out the window, the trees are a heavy black and the sky just blueing at 5:45. There's a hint of peach down low.

---

* The editing of *Memoria*.

August 31, 2020

And there's another storm. Another flash of lightning. Nothing dull about this life except, sometimes, me. Having arrived, I search my bag for my sandwiches and don't find them, think again that I'm losing my mind, then realize they're already on the table. The common theme. What would make me want to throw in the towel?

For a minute I wonder if noise could kill me. I could just sit here in the cabin and let the freeway's whistling cars pummel me with a thousand strokes a minute.

I think of how, when Michael* explains his choices for an edit, he uses the language of grammar and I don't know what he's talking about. I mean, not a clue. Nothing I've "learned" has stayed in my mind. I no longer know the mechanics of this art that I practice. It could be a metaphor for this experience, and perhaps for the time to come.

The rain and everything else has stopped now at 5:41. My weird thoughts too. An adjustment was made. Made unto me. Everything is clear again. The rain falls, the tires flap, the breeze flutters on my skin, my face in its reflection in the window, poor old face that it is, feeling and looking... chapped. I left Vaseline on overnight, and this morning, for the first time, didn't wash my face. I just let it be. Maybe that started my musing. Like a recognition, it signaled that I'm going to be cranky with aging, and not only with its physical aspects. I'm going to know less, not more. Something like that.

And I think... okay. Okay.

Fall apart, flake away, know nothing.

---

* Michael Mark assisted me with the editing of *Metanoia*.

Okay.

Let my sensitivities drift with the breeze, away from the hurts, a slow falling away of their contemplation, of their "place" in me.

This morning they could be gone. I realize they could be gone. What a wonder. Even moments without them "there," there in memory and cells, carries me elsewhere.

My single parenting: You have to do everything yourself (but you can't), and you have to depend on people (which you also can't) because it's all up to you and you're going to fail (and you can't fail your children).

I can bring it all back in an instant: the "it's all up to me" feeling, even when I know with absolute innocence that this breakdown of "what is up to me" has been happening since I first spoke with my angel, Peace.* A Holy "accompaniment" through life is real, and present in me... in that... "It is me, and It is more than me."

And dang if it isn't happening now with the editing. That feeling: It's all up to me. It's so strong, by which I mean that if the book goes out with errors it's on me. No matter how much help I get, it still comes back to me, my responsibility—it is "mine to do" because it was given to me to do.

So please help me, (and Michael), you "givers" of this "wonder" that I now want to carry lightly . . . with the child, my inner child's unknown knowing, my inner child before trauma. Erase the trauma . . . without erasing me. I let you wash it away outside of my viewing.

And I wish you would talk with me for a minute. I feel far away from speaking with you so naturally as I have for years of mornings. My work on manifesting our Way of Mary does this to me. It's like

---

* See *Peace*, Book 3 of The Grace Trilogy

it takes something away, even while I know I retain my sacred privacy, my inner sanctuary. I could remind myself of that more.

We will assist you in remembering. Do not worry. You have undone something this morning that we will not name.

September 1, 2020

I put my ear protection on and find it works better than it used to. Almost all sound is gone because I don't hear as well as I once did. And it's okay.

Our writing from yesterday stuns me because it sounds like the "real thing" and the writing I want to do. It reminded me of soliloquies I've read from other women. A former teacher, Meridel Le Sueur* comes to mind, although she's brilliant and I'm not. I am . . . something else.

Maybe I was right for this work *because* I am something else.

Maybe that will be the title of my memoir some day: "Something Else."

In a world of voices, we could so easily lose our own and forget our capacity to unite in Voice. To be operas of love's arias. Canticles of individuality.

To praise . . . personally.

Oh, my Lord and Mother, the day matches my writerly mood so perfectly. It is twilight dark in morning's glow. It's my every dream.

---

* Meridel Le Sueur was a writer first and foremost. Over the course of her life she wrote one hundred and thirty-three journals as well as children's books, works of fiction, non-fiction and poetry. She was an activist on behalf of women as well as the working class. See https://meridellesueur.org/.

With it I breathe freely. And it's still too dark to edit. Thank the Lord. Praise you, Mother.

Had a most wonderful conversation with Lee Flynn yesterday about the piece I sent him from *Memoria*. I was so blown away by the way I "re-saw" the end of Revelations, that I called him, and sent it to him.

He said, "It is so rich."

Yes. That's what he and I look for. A certain richness. The need to ponder.

Who really wants anything spelled out?

Lee and I love the mystery of the ponderable. The endlessly ponderable. Where we can place our gaze and have it returned and returned. Newer and newer. Never old. An ancient newness that disrupts time. What a life—to ponder the Imponderable, and then to meet It in the pondering.

Now the day has a twilight glow with dawn's hues. It's golden and dim. Low light. With my hearing protection, low noise. The coming of day before day is what I need, a person like me, who has no borders and is being relieved of pain.

I realize my thumb aches more on the left than the right because for years I've used my left thumb to hold my head up. I write and then I move in close to the screen, and with my thumb propping up my head, I read and ponder. Or read and edit.

I never knew I did it.

My body's memory so wants to keep doing it. That's the memory we're erasing isn't it . . . the memory of our bodies? Body memory. At least those where the hurts come or the traumas are held.

I am so in love with my moth friend. As she crosses the salt lamp like an eagle soaring over a mountain I have a sense, suddenly, that you're speaking of a greater "we," but please, today, just help me with finishing the edits.

October 30, 2020

I read on my phone before I am out of bed (a first) that the coronavirus affects the electromagnetic nature of the brain. Christina would know what that means in ways I don't. Maybe many things are combining to give us fuzzy brain. How does consciousness change on a vast scale? Change before it's too late?

The sky has changed now. There is a swath of dark blue sitting like a continent in the sky.

Transfiguration

November 2, 2020

Mirari is off, being readied for publication and a launch on Amazon. Michael is rereading it so that he can write a review and told me he had an experience, Mother! He felt a sensation in his gut, something he couldn't describe, and looked up and saw a hawk! What a marvel he is.

Oh, the wonder of it all!

Now I've wondered (ha!) *wandered* off again and come back at 6:36 to be with you and me one more time. Wondering and wandering. That's how it is. One time and one time and one time. In this moment of time in eternity all is still, the sky has lightened to a sweet dim blue and a very soft radiance is rising from behind the fence as if coming up from the bottom of the world. And, you know, Mother, I think I'm beginning to really love what I don't know. Maybe that's all any sort of quest is—a quest for what you don't yet know, where you haven't yet been, what you haven't yet felt.

Which is why, sweet love, you have to leave the past behind, particularly your past with A Course of Love. *You have written most of it "out" now. That is how "you" do it. That is how you come to peace with the past. You can't let it go until you have let it age and mellow along with you, which you do by writing it out and out and out. As many pages as the Way of the Marys will eventually be, you have written the same or more to work "out of you" what came in with your experience of* A Course of Love. *You look at your experience with*

Jesus in one way, and what you shared with those who didn't understand, in another.

To do something so many don't understand takes a lot of courage.

But this, Metanoia's turnaround, is a transfiguration. You have changed your view of events from the outer to the inner, and in doing so you now are beginning to exalt rather than denigrate the past. You may not think you do this yet, but you do. The appearance of our work, and your own appearance in the world are happening together.

That is so beautiful and hopeful to imagine, and I even feel it may be true.

You write it "out" to see it, and you now see that "this time" is not "that time." The old time is over. This is a new time.

You could be—of course *are*—right. It's a very strange feeling. I can see that very soon "the way it was" won't bother me in the slightest, and that pleases me, gives me the feeling of being in "no time." Being "over" time. Being one with time's nature is, in a way, being done with "the old."

It is a very noisy morning, with traffic working overtime. Ha! Yep, the traffic gives time a working over, compressing it into "rush hours" with all their fury.

To live here—"hearing the rush" but without the rush; being here in no-time even with the sound and fury of time—how good that could be, and how close it is to being! You have calmed me once again, Mother.

I want to assure you that in this time, "you" know best. You must only realize that you are still not ready to be done "re-writing" the past, and this is where we are taking you—to the freedom to leave be, or the freedom to create anew. "Going back" diminishes your sense of the place at which you have arrived. There is no "going back," and these words are speaking to you. I have spoken them to you. Today is about realizing further that this has occurred. It is okay, Mari, that you take from the past what is a springboard to going further into The New. But this time is almost over. You can be done with it, or you can linger in its familiarity . . . which is what most will do.

November 5, 2020

I'm not sure what reminded me of this quote from Robert Louis Stevenson—maybe the idea of choice—but it feels fitting: "To know what you prefer instead of humbly saying Amen to what the world tells you you should prefer, is to have kept your soul alive."

At 6:33, the barest, eye-straining level of distinction is coming to the yard and the warm glow of dawn has risen across the fence line.

November 6, 2020

Geese just flew by as I began to hear your voice telling me "I am" anchoring The New, and that this is why I am so tired. Thank you, Mother.

More graphically, dear heart, you are in the labor of the birth. The babe has taken everything from you. It will continue to do so until it is delivered and weaned. And what does this do? This time? It bonds you. The life you are bringing into the world bonds to you and bonds you to the world through it. You will stick around for it as long as you can because your lives are tied together.

But you have also been coming to know the error of trying too hard to take care of the child for too long. This time will be different. It is already different. The women in the circle* are to be your support, along with those men of the balanced feminine and masculine whom you call friends. Many more are already there but haven't "joined" you yet. You must discern if you want to be joined or if you want to retire to your hermitage—a decision you, in many ways, have already made.

November 7, 2020

I was just visited by a deer, Mother. He's a big fellow—too big to be the last one I saw. We looked at each other a long time. First, he came out of the woods and went toward the yard. Then he stood, blended with the trees so that if I hadn't known he was there I'd not have seen him. I said, "Oh, come back this way. I love you," and he twitched his tail and turned around. He strolled down the path towards the cabin, then stopped and looked in at me. After a moment, he continued his walk, passing out of my vision until he appeared again in the window, at the place where the squirrels usually feed. Finally, he made his way past the back of the cabin. Maybe this sign of gentleness is telling me that my work and I can be delivered gently.

---

* see *Mirari*, p. 13

Couplings

November 8, 2020

As I walked out to the cabin, the crows circled and circled and I stood, looking up at them from the path, the sky so purely blue, the denuded trees so sovereign and spectacular in their singularity they seemed to mark the day. *Mirari* is about to be published, *Memoria* is awaiting my edit, and we are just at the beginning here, of *Metanoia*.

"Revealed order" leaves "ordered time" behind. The revealed is always moving to the union and relationship that is life—that is giving and receiving as one. The life of Jesus interrupted ordinal time. You were told that "you and Mary" would have something to do with the end of ordinal time. Here you will see that while your Mary Love has moved you to much, this was also an announcement of your time with me, with the Way of Mary, and the coming of the time of the Marys. You and me, as she and Mary Magdalene, relate in the space of light with the unpredictable and elemental. We unite with singularities and enter relationships one-to-one. What we "bring in," through the couplings that we enter, will culminate in the final days of ordinal time and the Advent of The New.

RECEIVE INSTEAD OF PLAN

November 10, 2020

Today, I spoke with Christina, who had designs on changing my Amazon description and who was so reassuring that I just fell under her spell. Then she told me—my "Christina of the brilliant mind"—that she is not going to any grocery store other than the Whole Foods just a block away, that driving even there is nearly "too much," and that she has to tack notes to everything so she remembers what she needs to do. So now what's been happening with me doesn't feel so worrisome. We are comrades in experiencing The New in time, weird as it is. She calls these things "ascension symptoms."

November 13, 2020

It's fun to watch a squirrel, to see him find his nut and then determine just the right spot to sit undisturbed to eat it. It's very sweet really, that this particular one is sitting looking right at me. I always feel that as a sign of thankfulness. Then a blue jay comes along and tries to disturb him and he moves off his perch, but keeps his nut. He appears to bury it in the snow at the crook of the maple tree's trunk. That's his instinct.

I still need to trust my instinct more, don't I Mary?
Trust your treasure. Trust your nuts!

Remember orientation and disorientation, my Mari. But remember mainly that you are free. You are a day or so away from presenting Mirari: The Way of the Marys *to the world. And yes, I know you are doubtful. It is as "natural" to you to be so as it is to almost every other author in the world, especially those writing with any new ideas or self-exposure. You "felt" exposed with* ACOL, *but no one knew your story, and so it was a lesser revealing. Here you are at the beginning of a revealing that is in many ways a new story. Life—your life, the lives of your friends, the lives of women and men who come to our way—this is what is to be revealed. You are a good "friend." Not a savior in the old way but in the new way of friendship that is as old as time itself. "You are each other's own."*

You have given what will reveal this to some and not to others. You have done this with me. And we are just beginning. We will continue as long as you are comfortable doing so, and we will continue even if you return to your more "creative" writing, within which you will feel me as inspiration and as calls to rest.

Thank you, Mary. That is reassuring.

The "rush" is over now, and you have just gained the experience to know not to rush again. "Receiving instead of planning" can continue, even when you enter production, if you rest and wait for the inspiration of the "right time."

Ripening

I have discovered Martin Buber! This excerpt* is from his classic book *I and Thou*:

[T]here is a qualitative difference between historical ages. There are times of ripening when the true element of the human spirit, held down and buried, grows ready underground with such pressure and such tension that it merely waits to be touched by one who will touch it—and then erupts. The revelation that then appears seizes the whole ready element in all its suchness, recasts it and produces a form, a new form of God in the world.

Ever new regions of the world and the spirit are thus lifted up into form, called to divine form, in the course of history, in the transformations of the human element. Ever new spheres become the place of a theophany. It is not man's own power that is at work here, neither is it merely God passing through; it is a mixture of the divine with the human. Whoever is sent forth in a revelation takes with him in his eyes an image of God; however supra-sensible it may be, he takes it along in the eyes of his spirit, in the altogether not metaphorical but entirely real visual power of his spirit. The spirit also answers by beholding, a form-giving beholding. Although we on earth never behold God without world but only the world in God, by beholding we eternally form God's form.

---

* Buber, Martin. *I and Thou*. Translated by Walter Kaufmann, Touchstone, 1971, pp. 166-7.

This is what I "opened" to Lord and Mother. "A mixture of the divine with the human," and Oh, my living God! "A form-giving beholding." I feel so validated, but moreso, accompanied—accompanied through the ages by the ageless, living word.

Thank you, thank you my holy ones for this gift, and thank you Martin Buber. He says eloquently what I try to say plainly so that I can understand my own life, and I feel it has taken our entire book to say what Buber said in paragraphs.

My Mari, many will relate even more to words they hear from within your ordinary life, and you're not to take personally those who don't.

Having read more, he (Buber) says everything I would say. There is a relief in me over it . . . like finding another kindred spirit . . . much in the way I found Merton as an exemplar of my early desire to find solitude and be a hermit.

ℛEVELATION IS YOUR HERITAGE

Mother, I'm really beginning to see that what I've heard from both you and Jesus was never learned, rarely remembered "consciously," and yet is still in me. I've squirmed so many times because readers of my work remember more of what is in my books than I do, but I'm starting to realize that what is being lived—being lived through me somehow—is like a communion, in memory, of inner and outer. Memory exists in me but comes and goes from consciousness. It lets go and remembers, remembers and lets go, and doesn't (often to my chagrin) arise "as I" feel a need for it to do so.

I don't know that I've ever become aware of "a total change" in me, Mary, but I have changed greatly, especially my memory. And I believe it's possible that I have passed through "what the past seemed to teach me."[*]

I'm "aware" of an alteration I don't understand, can't grasp, and to which I have next to no intellectual capacities to bring to bear. Still, I've come to feel this sense of "who knows?" Who can know that a major change has come until it has actually moved into being? Becoming aware of those changes that are related to a new future is what I believe we're speaking of now, and if my own experience is any indication, it may be an unending . . . happening.

Over and over again, you and your fellow receivers of A Course of Love *will find yourselves reviewing what the past "but seemed" to teach you. This happens because your Brother gave you a "living Course." It follows your life. In this way you have been shown:* **Only**

---

[*] *ACOL* T3:10.7

"you" can follow love's course "in you." *This knowing is what has made space for our Way of Mary.*

ℛEVELATION IS KNOWING SHARED

Now that Mirari *has found its way into the world, and* Memoria *is being edited, I bring you back from external production to the internal "reception" of what you've been given. Here, you begin to realize you've come back different than when you left. One manner in which we can speak of this difference is in regard to "doing."*

You have not realized this, but the "sharing" that is the mode of the revolutionized consciousness, is not something you "do." The written word we share comes of abiding in a manner of consciousness that is open and responsive. In this unrestricted and receptive consciousness, what is received comes to you and extends from you, much like the miracle of birth.

When you write you create The New. Writing is an unrepeatable act of creation.

"Our" writing comes of recognition of a shared life force. While the nature of giving and receiving being one in truth applies here, it also has lagged behind due to your hierarchical understanding of one who gives and one who receives. Sharing (rather than doing) is what comes "after" the change. **Shared knowing is revelation. It is the "new knowing." Revelation is knowing shared.** But it's not knowing in the manner you have come to expect. It is neither individual nor collective. It is knowing that exists in every living, being, and changing particle of matter. It comes forward naturally (unless you block it) and invites The New into being.

In our dialogue, it is as though all around you has been noise, and now quiet has come. When you have stilled every inquiry, you watch your hand move. Your hands are delicate. They travel in a pattern *across your keyboard. You pick up your cup and raise your chin toward the sun, even while your eyes remain on our words. You lower your cup. Your eyes close. You open them.*

You have partaken of what you see, as you partake of what you have touched. So, too, is it with our words. The way you take in Holy Words is little different than the way you reach or sip or gaze. All of it is a physical, personal, and consciously unconscious experience because it is natural.

You cannot understand your Self objectively. You are not objects and cannot be reduced to your constituent parts. Consciousness stands as the source, the origin, and the basis of everything. Everything!

THE POWER OF BEING

Breaking the Barriers of Conventional Knowing: Being Affected

You and I both know that it's hard for you to come back to receiving after being in the production mode you entered to ready Memoria *for publication.*

That's true. They are two vastly different ways of being—the latter ruled by skills I have a much harder time with now.

As you return to the "receiving" by which we compose this narrative of The New, it's the right time to speak of receiving itself . . . here . . . as we begin again. Receiving is "always" a shared knowing, the very knowing whose time has come. It arrives in many ways beyond that which we, together, bring forth. It was two decades between the release of A Course of Love *and* Mirari: The Way of the Marys, *even though you and your Jesus had a great many conversations in that time.*

Yes, that's true. These dialogues of the Way of the Marys were "our" beginning.

And our first encounter in 2013 prepared you. Dialogues are always a mutually receptive activity. What comes of them now is powered by a revolutionized consciousness. Everything you "receive" in this way comes from the one-to-one realm of no use—including the writing you publish, the writing that will affect many in the same one-to-one manner. They, like you, will find within it that which cannot be used. This is the difference in our intimate feminine dialogue: It cannot be misappropriated. That's because it is personal.

While it is a critical time to see that all such works, whether they seem to be so or not, are personal as well as universal (and meant to be that way for each), this is not the major reason we speak in this way. There really is no "reason" other than that it is the natural feminine way. It also signifies why I could never speak to you in the manner that Yeshua did. It would have been unnatural for me.

Your Jesus has this feminine side as well. You treasure your personal writings with Him, in your journals and what you call The Jesus Chronicles,* *in a different way than you do* A Course of Love, *because of this, don't you?*

Yes, now that you say it, I realize that I do, and always have. But I felt great love in *A Course of Love*, too, especially in "The Embrace."

In the same way, you treasure what "you" knew of A Course of Love *for having received it as a participant, even though it wasn't always obvious in the work.*

That's true as well.

And that's the personal. **It is a personal experience to be affected.** *Teaching can easily obscure this truth. Those who want to keep matters objective and impersonal further a limited way. Many were touched by* A Course in Miracles *and* A Course of Love *in ways they didn't understand until they began to "live" it. In a sense, they were the lucky ones. Many others remained attached to arriving at a preselected destination. This is their way of dealing with things. Because people do "deal" with things. Those we touch are no longer doing this. They are ready, and from them, more and more will become ready, to be done with ways of "dealing," which has its root in division. They may not realize they have been readied to be done*

---

* These personal conversations between Mari and Jesus were preserved, and portions are available as "The Jesus Chronicles" at www.mariperron.com.

seeking, or done "using and being used," or done being divided from their own knowing, but this is what occurs.

This is what ACIM and ACOL started. This is the way of increase and multiplication in this revolutionary time that is breaking the barriers of conventional knowing—transcending a way of knowing that primarily seeks to use knowledge to achieve an agreed upon end. Those who teach, and many who learn from teachers, paint themselves into boxes of agreement that they believe enable "getting somewhere." They bring many with them, and with the destination established, may arrive at a location that frees them more from joy in their human experience than from learning.

Still, this revolutionary and evolutionary time "is" breaking down the barriers of conventional knowing and established knowledge. You cannot even begin to conceive of the necessity of this breakthrough or all that will come of it.

Even when I can't see it happening?

Even when you can't see it happening. Yes. But while you don't see it in "many," and don't see it in the public sphere, you are seeing it in many beautiful souls, of whom there are far more than you are aware. It is all as simple and complex as the recognition of soul that you long to see in the eyes as clearly as you see it in the rising of each day.

We do not speak intimately only for your benefit. Intimacy is the realm of soul, and it is the soul's private and personal reach that can break these dams of "the mind's" convention, ridding those who come to us of their preconceived notions of what they believe they want to know, and how they believe they come to know it. We do this because it is "what" they want to know, and "how" they believe they know it, that has obscured their souls.

Metanoia sparks the revolutionary change that brings each of you into an acceptance of "your" way of knowing, which in turn invites the imaginal. If you look back at your time of receiving A Course of Love, *Mari, you will see it had begun already, not only in your acquaintance with the imaginal but with the way it changed your "thinking mind."*

Jesus obliquely alerted you that this was coming when you heard, prior to your reception of ACOL, *that you couldn't go on with your "thinking mind." You saw this, then, as a suggestion that you needed to get yourself out of the way, to move aside for what Jesus was bringing in. This was why you were paused, and why your return occurred within The Embrace.* You were able to discover for yourself that you weren't being asked to get "your self" out of the way, but to be your full self, a true self devoid of ego and present to feelings. You were becoming aware that what Jesus asked of you—this letting go of the thinking mind—was being asked of all. This period changed you and changed your experience.*

You were literally stopped so that you could see this. Ever since, you have struggled to carry on with all that is of the thinking mind, especially facets of time and learning that are linear and detail-oriented. The feminine energy isn't linear. It is imaginal at its core. So, you can see why we must take a new route to move you, and many—men and women—away from the prized assets of the time that is passing.

The thinking mind is like an insanely jealous lover who doesn't want you to turn to anyone or anything else. The innovation and excitement of new ideas or areas of interest are almost always met by

---

* A pause in my receiving occurred between Chapters 19 and 20 of *A Course of Love*. Chapter 20 is entitled "The Embrace."

"No" before they come to "Yes," and the truly new comes to "Yes" primarily because the idea, or felt knowing, won't leave "you" alone.

I can testify to that. I had to pause a minute before I realized it, but the pause made me so happy. Yes! I want ideas that won't leave me alone, like I want the bunnies and birds who await their feed. I love the feeling of being awaited and of being helpful in my way as much as I love the feeling of new knowing awaiting me.

That's my Mari. Thank you for coming back to me. Now is the time to delve further into this most miraculous of your experiences and to free you from aspects of your past that still haunt you. This period was pivotal.

You're speaking of the period before I received "The Embrace."

Yes.

That was when, after hearing Jesus' words unfailingly each time I sat ready to do so, I first experienced silence. I heard nothing. I was in such a panic that I don't even remember going back to what I had just received (Chapter 19). The cause of my great despair as I sat, awaiting Jesus—day after day for the next ten weeks—was wondering what I had "done wrong" for the stoppage to occur.

You felt like you were being punished?

I don't think I'd put it that harshly, Holy One. I didn't "blame" Jesus. I blamed myself.

And by that you mean you were punishing yourself?

Well, I was looking for *reasons* in myself. And one that I sensed was part of it, was that my receiving had become like a "job" I was here to do. So, it brought up all those feelings of not measuring up to the job, of somehow falling short. I had my little working group waiting for each installment, and that added to my drivenness and the work-like feeling.

I don't often do that anymore, Mother. I don't share before I'm ready. I wait until I'm done or just send a piece that I feel will really touch one of my friends. That pressure was an awful feeling.

But it was more than that.

Yes. There was also a more underground feeling that I couldn't quite look at, but that was the one affecting me the most. I suppose I couldn't see it while I was worrying over things. And I didn't want to see it.

Tell me, now, my daughter.

I think it was, ultimately, that it—the receiving—was beyond my control and, at the same time, dependent on me. This made me feel very fragile.

Your course from Jesus was the babe of your womb.

Oh, Mary. Yes. If I couldn't see it through (and now I'm choking up) the new babe wouldn't come to be. And no one could do it for me. It was "in me already." It couldn't be taken out and given to another to raise. It was both out of my control and dependent on me. Just like being pregnant. And I couldn't abort it.

It mirrored the hardest and most vulnerable times of your life.

Yes.

And during those times, when you sought support for yourself, you felt that you "lowered yourself" to appeal for this support, and even then it was denied.

Mary, this is really hard. I wasn't expecting this. The pain is too great.

Tell me.

The Support That Didn't Come

I close my eyes, scenes flashing through my memory. Then I begin.

While my first two pregnancies weren't ideal, the third was devastating. I felt like I knew what I had to do, but when I tried, I couldn't go through with it: an abortion. I then called the man who was the father, telling him I wanted to talk in person. He picked me up and we drove in his red and black Chevy Nova, which he prized, to Harriet Island to sit by the Mississippi River. It was 1978 and I was 23 years old.

Still sitting in the car, I told him of the pregnancy and said, "I want you to marry me, or at the very least to get engaged and commit to helping me." I asked that of him because, I thought, then I wouldn't be alone, and even engagement would help to still the shudders of all who knew me and who would think how stupid I was to let myself get pregnant again. I hated being seen as stupid.

It was so hard to ask.

And then he told me he was marrying someone else.

Just like that. A simple statement. "I'm marrying someone else." It took my breath away.

In my shock, I began to cry and turned my head. Looking out the window and away from him and the river, I don't know how much time went by. I would have liked to be looking at the river, but he was on that side of the car, and I couldn't look at him.

When I finally turned back and spoke, the words forgotten now, he didn't answer. His head was turned away from me, so I sat forward in my seat and saw that he had fallen asleep. There was drool in the corner of his mouth.

That he could sleep! That was how little it concerned him? The pain was almost too much to bear. I got out of the car and walked home, a couple of miles up steep hills. And then I hid the pregnancy as long as I could, so fearful of those looks, those words that would just hurt me again and again. "How could you be so stupid?"

I'm rocking you as you cry. And we're almost done. It was a hard pregnancy, and you were hospitalized at seven months. You almost lost her, your Angela. But almost losing her made you want her and cherish her. And then this child of your fiercest sorrow, and your gentlest love, came to be your second greatest challenge next to A Course of Love. *Your greatest sacrifices and your greatest pain—held together.*

Yes.

And then you came to voice.

𝒜 REVOLUTION
THAT HONORS THE PAIN

And now that you have slept on this—now that you have ceased to minimize the pain—now that you can look instead at your courage and strength of heart, are you ready to move forward without your default pattern? Your pattern of looking at "the situation" apart from your own self and feelings? Of looking at what others think, while you focus on surviving? On what you need "to do"? Can you see the missing step of self-love?

I see that every time I *was* looking out for myself, trying to love myself, I got shot down.

And that kept you at merely trying to survive, rather than to thrive.

Well, that's true enough. Aside from the years when I worked at the University of Minnesota, my whole life as a young adult revolved around survival.* And Donny and I have had some lean years, too, Mother. But it's okay. Other than for "this." This has been hard on me. Necessary, I can see that, but hard. It's like being consumed by the inner, with nothing left for the outer.

And yet you've had such encouraging signs. Everyone you speak to has been remarking on your difference, your laughter, your spiritedness. And you have felt your courage and power rising up.

You're right. It's just this last piece that's been so challenging. I kept thinking it was done, but it wasn't done, and I couldn't "figure out" what was needed.

---

* I left my job at the University of Minnesota in response to the call that soon became *A Course of Love*.

And now you know. There is only one more piece. The time of The Embrace. Let's finish it up.

𝒯HE LEGACY OF TRAUMA AND MY RETURN TO VOICE

When my receiving of *A Course of Love* was paused after Chapter 19, the only failure I couldn't attack with my "doing" tendencies was my body's failure. I became an emotional mess, overwhelmed by all kinds of feelings I couldn't make sense of. I went to the doctor and found I was anemic and menopausal. I wasn't expecting either.

I got what assistance I could for the physical side of things, and then appealed to Mary Love and Julieanne Carver[*] for their help in understanding the implications of a vision I had received.[†] I had a feeling it was linked to my decline. It was a vision of myself in a cave.

We met at Mary's home in her writing room, where she and Julie had me lay on the daybed as they invoked their united power to call me out of the cave. That poor woman (me) just did not want to move. She wanted to stay where she was. And then I heard "that me" who was in the cave say, "I have no voice here," and only for that reason did she begin to feel more like me, and I made the decision to come out. I came out, knowing that I was coming out, and coming "back," to have a voice.

Tell me the rest of it, my daughter. The "scene" behind it was significant and you have bypassed it.

That's true, I have. But I don't think it has anything to do with *A Course of Love*. And . . .

---

[*] Julieanne was a colleague at the University of Minnesota, and co-author of *Love*, the first book of *The Grace Trilogy*.

[†] See *Mirari*, p. 30.

You've never put much stock in past life visions?

It's one of those things that I hope won't happen to our words, Mary. Past lives were such a topic of interest at that time, and overused. Everyone who talked about them had once been someone famous.

I understand. But you weren't anyone famous.

No. I was being stoned . . . for some indiscretion with a man I loved. By my attire and the environment in which I ran, I believe I was in a place and time like your own. I was running from the crowd, and the stones, and saw an opening in a cave ahead. I ran into it, and stones began to fall from the inside, sealing the entrance.

Later, after the crowd had gone, perhaps the next day, the man I loved came to the cave, crying, carrying-on like a part of him knew I was alive in there. He was calling out to me. He talked to himself, too, telling himself he was foolish to believe it. And I "chose" not to answer. If I had, he might have been able to dig me out. But I did not want to "come out."

That was the end of what you could see of that life, but I have told you that you lived on.

Yes, and I can imagine easily why that "me" felt she would be happier alone in a cave than she was in the judging eyes and danger of the crowd.

And could you suppose that this still affects you and your choices now?

I've never had an investigatory yen toward it, Mother, and so, not being drawn, I have been content with not knowing more than that. It felt like enough to learn about it with Mary and Julie and to know it was about having a voice. That was what made it feel true . . . and ordinary. I wasn't anyone special. I was a common woman who became a forager, somehow finding a way to stay alive and out of view for a time. But through their inquiry, I came to see it much like my yen for solitude and my contrary need to have a voice. I'd bet many writers feel the same way. We don't exactly want to "go public," even though, at the same time, we do desire to see our message shared with the world.

You couldn't imagine how much I struggled over leaving my job, where I worked with my best friends, with a great boss, had seniority and was making money. But I didn't think I could write "a new course in miracles" if I stayed. This was beyond my wildest imaginings.

It was after the writing got going that I felt I needed some sort of partnership, and invited my friend Dan to be that partner. Unfortunately, he soon felt more like the boss of me. He was "a name" in the book business and so the book people, like Marc Allen*, gravitated toward him. Pretty soon I wasn't even consulted before decisions were made.

It's not unusual. It's the way publishing works. But it's also why I'm publishing our books myself now.

Keeping to myself, as I needed to do with so many situations . . . from family, to writing, to relationships, I know I lost some chances for intimacy—but I survived Mary.

And that's still your default position. Survival.

It's another legacy of that life in Turkey. Are you willing to believe that you were there in Turkey, and that when my spiritual gaze met yours, you could feel that I was "for you"? So that you were no longer torn between two lives, as you had been? And as you are now?

---

* *ACOL*'s first publisher, with New World Library.

Oh, Mother, this feels like too much. I do not feel ready for this or to uproot my life.

I do not ask you to be uprooted, my daughter, no. But I do ask you to see that the sources of your pain are greater than you have viewed them. Because this story of great pain "to you" was repeated in recent years, and some might not otherwise see it as being great enough to have wounded you as much as it did. And this matters to you, even when you say it doesn't. Life's continuum allows for healing and safety and the feeling of others being "for you" when you look honestly at "all" the causes of the pain, my Mari. And . . . all the minimizing of pain. It is a key to why you still are uncertain of having a voice.

Yes, I can see where that could be true.

I have noticed many "scenes" flashing in and out of memory. I often remember my last view of Mary Magdalene, which was through spiritual vision. She was in a cave like the one you mention, and I will tell you that there is a connection.

You chose the name Magdalene as your confirmation name, partially because, although your mother went by "Madeline," her birth name was Mary Magdalene. With your birth name being Margaret Mary, you would be Margaret Mary Magdalene. You also chose partially for your identification with the biblical story of Mary Magdalene as the fallen woman. You were still an innocent, but there was something in you that knew you would not be an innocent for long, wasn't there?

Yes! And I don't know why. I never knew why. Really, all the girls I knew in grade school were truly nice, and even kind. I switched to a new school, St. Matthews, in fifth grade, where I knew only one person—a neighborhood girl, Maureen Clancy. I had previously been attending St. Adalbert's, a small school where everyone knew me as well as my older brothers and sister. But when my older sister graduated, my parents thought it would be better if I went to a school closer to home. The first year was hard. I think by seventh or eighth grade I had a few good friends who remained into my first years of high school. But that changed too.

I became disillusioned after the sophomore retreat because everyone "got real" and then, back at school, went right back to being hidden. It broke my heart, really. That's when I decided to change schools again (this time of my own volition). The memory inspired me to look at my sophomore yearbook, and there were two who, when signing it, spoke of my bravery. But even they couldn't persuade me to stay.

While I was still shy about boys, I did want them to be attracted to me . . . more than I wanted girlfriends. I can remember, in those first years of high school,* thinking I wanted a boyfriend so that I would have someone who was "for me." I don't think I imagined true love necessarily, and not sex either, just someone who was—and those were my exact words—"for me." My sister, who is five years older, grew up before my eyes with a boyfriend in a time when you went steady and went to proms, and your boyfriend was "yours." I came of age in an opposite time that scoffed at such attachments.

It was a time of very abrupt change, I know. And so, all those dreams you had were met by a different reality.

Yes.

Ah. Are you seeing the common thread?

Yes. And I have tears in my eyes.

---

* My high school years were 1968 – 1972.

You grew into adulthood without that, didn't you? Without having someone who was "for you."

Yes.

And now perhaps you can see why the wounds that were to come with your Course of Love *went so deep?*

Yes! Those I thought would be "for me" were not "for me."

There you go. This isn't a twenty-year wound but a wound of fifty years, and if you were to count the woman who helped you remember you wanted a voice, you could speak of centuries. This wound of life is a memory of failure "to connect" that goes to the heart of all time, including this time. Many suffer in this way, and women still often remain unsure of having a voice . . . especially when it matters.

Oh, my Mother, as we're speaking, I notice that I have a wounded squirrel feeding on the similarly wounded but newly growing maple tree. The squirrel keeps falling over and looks so helpless. I believe it may be an injury to her right rear leg. I'll watch out for her as much as I can.

I try to watch out for myself now, too, Mary. And truly, I have no right to complain. I have far more than a few true connections now. Some are with people I don't see often, but they are more amazing than I would ever have imagined.

And at home your "all" has been "here," in creative acts of the imagination that set you apart from the life of family.

Yes, and I do appreciate respect for that.

And yet you feel "like a big baby" when you are left out of family plans or activities.

Boy, you know everything, don't you! I suppose they feel I ignore them much of the time, and so sometimes, when I would join them if they asked, they don't. But Mother, my feelings *then* were so raw.

This is what you're getting at, I know. How I started to feel "left out" of my own work. I was only forty-three years old when it started. Although I probably felt in my prime then, now it feels young, and my body was going through the huge transition of menopause. I was exhausted and emptied, and at the same time, full to bursting with emotion. I felt loneliness, (I missed Mary and Julie a lot), and for a time I also moved between elation and confusion with the receiving.

And so, when Jesus finally returned and wrapped his arms around me and called me into his embrace and that of the imaginal realm, I was undone with gratefulness:

Your longing now has reached a fever pitch, a burning in your heart quite different from that which you have felt before. Your heart may even feel as if it is stretching outward, straining heavenward, near to bursting with its desire for union, a desire you do not understand but can surely feel.

This is a call to move now into my embrace and let yourself be comforted. Let the tears fall and the weight of your shoulders rest upon mine. Let me cradle your head against my breast as I stroke your hair and assure you that it will be all right. Realize that this is the whole world, the universe, the all of all in whose embrace you literally exist. Feel the gentleness and the love. Drink in the safety and the rest. Close your eyes and begin to see with an imagination that is beyond thought and words.*

From here your life becomes imaginal, a dream that requires you not to leave your home, your place of safety and of rest. You are

---

* *ACOL* C:20.1-2

cradled gently while your spirit soars, dreaming happy dreams at last. With love surrounding you in arms that hold you close, you feel the heartbeat of the world just beneath your resting head. It thunders in your ears and moves through you until there is no distinction. We are the heartbeat of the world.

This is creation. This is God. This is our home.*

When you returned to the group you were associated with then, having sent them this beautiful new chapter, you were very happy.

Yes, I returned overjoyed with the new material and just as thrilled that I was hearing again. I told them how comforted I was, and how it felt so personal. And do you know what my partner said? He said, "It's not about you, Mari. It's not personal."

---

* *ACOL* C:20.10-11

PRONOUNCEMENTS AND THEIR EFFECTS

I felt so slapped down. My eyes immediately began to sting with tears. And there was nowhere to hide. I went to the bathroom to try to regain my composure. But I didn't stay. I wasn't able to leave fast enough. I ached all over from trying to hold myself together until I could get out of there.

When I read *The Gospel of Mary Magdalene* many years later, a particular passage brought up my memory of this experience. Speaking of Peter, the author reveals that a "climate of jealousy" still holds him back, and his consequent mistrust of the feminine prevents him from reclaiming the missing parts of love.

"Faced with Peter's incomprehension," we hear that "Mary wept," and answered him: "My brother Peter, what can you be thinking? Do you believe that this is just my own imagination, that I invented this vision? Or do you believe that I would lie about our Teacher?"

The Commentary states that "... [Mary Magdalene's] tears are not the ones she knows best—those of grief, love, or awe—but the tears of a child before an adult who refuses to believe her at the very moment when she has opened her heart in truth."[*]

With my partner, I couldn't even say, as Mary Magdalene did, "What are you thinking?" And I wouldn't have thought of my tears as those of a child before an unbelieving adult, but that's a description that fits my experience too. I've shed tears for that

---

[*] Leloup, Jean-Yves. *The Gospel of Mary Magdalene*. Inner Traditions, 2002, p. 165.

reason many times. "Then," I was still vulnerable to pronouncements. For a while afterwards, I told myself, "Oh, yes, yes, he must be right. I'm wrong to feel the way I do." But I never really believed it.

And that's when the thing started, Mary. That was the beginning of the end of the old way for me, of letting people define my experience as if it was separate from me. I had to "own it" even when it felt like a secret I couldn't share. It's what made me as certain as I've been with you, Mary. I've understood I have to "claim" my own way here because I am "with you" in this, just as I was "with Jesus" in *ACOL*. Now that we've talked of it, I see I finally had someone who was for me! Jesus!

While Donny has been a wonderful supporter, even of me leaving my job, and understood far more than I gave him credit for, he couldn't assist me as a partner in this area. Although one time, when I was tortured enough to mention a change being put forward that I didn't want to make to *A Course of Love*, he said, "If you don't write it the way you heard it you won't be able to live with yourself." What a sign of knowing me those words were! I had to stand up for the voice of Jesus.

Dearest Mary, even though I had to make my own way with Jesus—which wasn't always easy—I couldn't feel more generous about sharing what has come of it than when I receive a heartfelt letter from a reader, as I just did. Then I can only say, "It's yours! It is spoken—every word—to your own heart!" I hope each person feels *A Course of Love* is "theirs" in the way I felt *A Course in Miracles* was "mine" as I read it. That's the way it is with the greatest of our holy literature. It's just that having this experience doesn't give anyone the right to assert a singular interpretation of these holy words, to make pronouncements about their ultimate meaning, or to claim an authority over them.

I can't imagine telling someone, "*It's not about you.*" I can still feel how hard that was on me. And it wasn't the only time it happened.

While no one could see my relationship with Jesus in *ACOL*, as mine with you can be seen here, it *felt* just as intimate. Jesus spoke to me in a cherished manner as I received His Course. Sometimes He advised me regarding it. We also shared conversations "outside" of those meant for *A Course of Love*, such as those I call *The Jesus Chronicles* as mentioned earlier.

This manner of being with each other is precisely what I intuit will be the way of The New, Mary. It's not about new interpretations or objective meanings! It has to do with holy relations and even holiness personified. *A Course of Love* was created to share love personally. Its way *is* intimate. It's not about some objective form of knowledge that exists apart from us, but who each of us are in union *and* relationship. Really, it's everything we're talking about now! *ACOL* and Metanoia are about The New.

The co-opting of our voices and ourselves is old. As old as time. It's not *only* the way of the spiritual but the way of commerce and professionalism. It goes by many names. It is where self-removal is expected. It is where the dominant ones (male or female, professor, or priest) tell other people what they ought to believe; how they should (or shouldn't) feel; or what they do and don't have as rights, including the right to protest. The way it happens in the arts is the same.

The mistreatment of women in much of your part of the world, Mary, can make me feel uneasy about speaking so emphatically of what happens artistically because there's so much brutality! But it's all tied together in some way. It's about who determines what is acceptable. To "dominate" is to rule or control by power *or* influence. That's a dictionary definition and I use it because of the word influence. How seldom do we think of the powerful as those able to influence "the many" to their view, their rules, or even to what they see as their right to break the rules.

  That's the bigger picture we're looking at now, Mary, the way I see it. I am only revealing my pain because you asked, and now I can see why. These things can feel, and are, so intimately personal . . . and then you look around and see how heartbreakingly universal the abuses have become. Those who seek to ban abortion never seem ready to meet the corresponding need to enforce child support, or fund daycare. How many men would be careless about getting a woman pregnant if they were made to support the child? How many women would keep a child they could afford to keep?

  Life is personal. Each reader of these works who "hears" them and takes them in—who is affected by them in *their own way*—will completely understand the personal nature of it for them, as well as for me. **Personal doesn't mean "exclusive"! Only individual and unique.** And the individual and unique is what makes us who we are and ought not be denied. That's all I'm saying. No one has the right to tell us what is or is not personal to us. It's with the intimacy that abides at the heart of us that we gain the capacity for "letting" words touch us at the feeling, rather than intellectual, level!

  The personal is what gives us the "both/and" view of me and you, each being affected distinctively, individually . . . in our own ways. It's the personal that grants us the ability to see and feel the relationship of self and divine . . . "together." That "togetherness" or "inseparableness" is the revelation that becomes Metanoia. Our revolution in consciousness grants us, each of us, access to the experience itself.

From here your *life becomes imaginal**... *that's the experience!*

Yes, Mary. That's where I was introduced to the imaginal. At that very early time in *A Course of Love*. Each of us who lets the revolution happen encounters this change in our own experience. Mine was of an upwelling and deeply personal energy, which made me *available* to the imaginal realm. "It," I believe, finds "us," when we're ready.

And what was happening to you then was that you were being made ready?

Yes. I think so.

Now, as you and I speak of Metanoia, my view is that it is, maybe, like attaining "the courage" that lets us welcome being doused with the whole of our story—the one we've lived and the one we're destined to live—until we're saturated with it. Whether we know what our story is or not, we have one, and it can't be extinguished. This work opens us to see that it will be shown to us if we but allow it. Being *in our own story* returns our authentic lives to us. It's why I couldn't let myself be "removed" from the space of communion I shared with Jesus.

What we live is of life's invitation—the offering, and our acceptance of it. That's the greatest part! The manner of our living invites each of us into, not only our own story, but a larger story that we share. I feel that you can't share it until you know it and you can't know it until you share it. It's confounding for a while because there's not really any "thing" to know. But we can know and share

---

* *ACOL* C:20.10

ourselves. And it's like "the offering" goes both ways and lets us see what is available, and that we need to *be available* if we are to encounter a revolutionized way of knowing.

All of it together makes it a shared story that is, paradoxically, our most intimate and true story. The all-inclusive story. Not only the imminently personal, but the soulful, and the divine, and the unitive story. These are stories of the lives we are here to live.

As were ours. And you just did what each of us did. We spoke our words so that we could hear them and share them. We spoke words so that we could heal. They came amongst us, as yours so often do amongst your friends. As we come to voice, we honor the pain. And as we honor our pain together, we prepare a room in each where their pain may be just as respected and illuminating as yours and mine have been.

I feel as if I can forgive now more than I ever have before.

Because we revealed your pain and *relieved you of your sources of shame. Can you see, daughter, why you have been susceptible to shame?*

Oh, yes. I don't think the "why" behind it has ever been further away than the blink of an eye. That susceptibility shuts and opens, opens and shuts. Shame is drawn up unawares, and easily, especially by those who are in power-over positions.

Because it's all on you.

I guess so, yes. But it just occurred to me that the way things were left with my writing, was the same sort of abandonment I felt with absentee fathers.

My dear heart, this is what I've been waiting for you to see . . . in your way . . . in your own right timing. Years ago, men left you to care for your babies alone. More recently, men sought to remove you from your place as birth mother of these works with us.

BEING A BIRTH MOTHER

There's a reason that my son, your Brother, called you to see yourself in this way—as the "birth mother" of his Course of Love—*a reason he called you to revisit this pain. He presaged your trials, your abandonment, and your discovery of your rightful place. Could you, now, begin to imagine that this was the quickest and most effective way for him to encourage you to stop abandoning your Self? To actually raise your self-esteem? You did not fight for your rights due to arrogance, but to gain proper self-respect. These hidden blessings allowed you to find the strength to claim, and honor, each child of your womb, including these you birth with us. Many, many women need to do this claiming before they can feel relief from the pains of "take-overs" in one or another area of their lives.*

Can you begin to imagine that I understand, as a woman who was very frightened and uncertain in being called upon to carry in my womb what no man had fathered? Can you not imagine that there were many who did not believe? Who wanted to shame me? Who spoke behind my back? Can you imagine what it was to allow the rest of my life to be designed "for me" around this child of my womb, including Yeshua's "adoptive" father? Much was taken out of my hands, as has happened with you, and Mary Magdalene had her own struggles.

But, as has also happened with you, Mary Magdalene took up her call as I took up mine. It had nothing to do with those who thought they knew the way. Nothing at all. "They" were completely immaterial to what we knew we needed to do. Can you see the perfection in my son's choice of you? It was, and is, a redeeming choice. You fell in love with his Course in Miracles *and he in love with you and Helen in a human way . . . just like he did during his time on Earth. He loved me as a mother. He loved Mary Magdalene and each of his disciples as the rest of his family on Earth. He loved the one now called "doubting Thomas" as greatly as the others but loved each in a particular way. His life offers the chance for many to take up the way of Thomas and Saul, which is to be redeemed—restored in truth, as they were.*

What any holy literature will tell you (no matter the difference in wording) is that "Whomever is in Christ is a new creation." And most will also tell you that when you have realized this and made it real, you are freed from "the pattern" that created all the others that, until now, chronicled the story of your life. You are then released to Creation of The New.

FEELING FOR YOURSELF

Pain, sorrow, sadness and suffering are most often feelings of compassion. Through empathy, you "come to" compassion, to feeling "with." When you are feeling sensitive over your own circumstances, you just aren't as likely to see the compassionate side of them, because you are feeling for yourself alone. "Feeling for yourself" (so often misrepresented as "feeling sorry for yourself") is finding your divinity through the immeasurable range of your psyche, of senses that are present to the inner, the outer, and the beyond of both the old and The New. Remember that being "here," we "set the old surroundings aside for the new surroundings."*

Part of your revolution in consciousness is realizing that you can have compassion for yourself "here." But what if we were to change your view in an even broader way? What if we were to speak of this as the rise of feelings that are of your soul, your soul who knows for you?

Remember how viscerally you felt when hearing our words spoken by Coralie, and while we are, together, "un-naming" much, the words we use still matter. As you heard in ACOL, *there will be a new language, a shared language:*

You will find that your new *language* will gather people to you in much the way people will gravitate toward beautiful music. ... [T]he memory of this *language* exists within them as well. It will come naturally to you to welcome these back to the common *language* of the mind and heart joined in unity. You will desire more than

---

* *Mirari*, p. 74

anything for everyone you encounter to share this remembered language.*

We are going even deeper here in changing human speech, changing not only thought and feelings but your expression of thought and feelings. Doing so is momentous. It will contribute to the revolution in consciousness that many are just beginning to sense. We want our words heard with vocal sounds, and the rush of the wind, the melody of The New, the "who/awe" of breath, and the heartbeat that rocks you.

What other language might your heart speak? It is a language spoken so quietly and with such gentleness that those who cannot come to stillness know it not. The language of your heart is the language of communion.†

Metanoia is not only a spiritual conversion but a power that changes one's mind. It speaks of that which causes a literal turn, a reorientation that completes your resurrection of memory and welcomes you to know again the wholeness, the fullness, and the wonder of the embrace.

The embrace can now be likened to the starting point of a shared language, a language shared by mind and heart and by all people . . . the language of images and concepts that touch the one heart and serve the one mind.‡

---

* *ACOL* C:10.15 (emphasis added)
† *ACOL* C:8.3
‡ *ACOL* C:21.6 (emphasis added)

You and your Jesus agreed, in A Course of Love, *that you would create a "new" language, and that you needed to start somewhere. Here that mission commences. We have started something. The time is "here" for the language of love's creative vision to leave its mark on the time that is coming into being.*

The Way of Mary
Breaking the Chain / Going Elsewhere

One purpose of all that has come to you is to break the chain of your training—the chain that keeps you silent when you need to speak.

That lifetime of training was so thorough that you don't recognize it without help. It has a hold on you. Many women feel this hesitancy. Metanoia is the innovation that frees you from it. This breakthrough has many presentations, only one of which is about voice.

The training told you to bring all you want, all you seek, all you fear, all that makes you sad, to your thinking mind. The training told you that your mind "is" you. You had nowhere else to go. All uniform and secular directions pointed there. All roads to the acceptance and praise each child needs and desires, are tied to varieties of fitting in, to grades, to achievement, to behavior and most poignantly, to acceptance. A compassionate parent or caring teacher, in the isolating world of instruction, often makes a huge difference. And so does belief.

Belief reveals an "elsewhere" in much the way love does, especially in an unkind, "fact and information" based environment.

Like art and nature, religion's greatest gift is that it opens children to wonder, to an idea of a greater reality than that of facts, and to a knowing that there is someplace other than the thinking mind where they can go. The imagination plays an incredible role in a child's connection to divine love, and even the "mystery of faith."

The name or style of the religion or practice doesn't matter, so long as children are not shamed or taught to judge by those who preach fundamentalism and fear. Many wars are caused by "one right way" thinking. But even this is not enough to dissuade the sense of God that naturally arises and is nurtured by an awareness—historic or otherwise—of God's presence.

"Awareness" is always an acknowledgment of something felt. The feeling that any "God of Love" inspires, is one for which no other source can account.

I do not deny that much of religion was taught in unkind ways that led to shame, but despite the faults of their elders, and sometimes because of them, many a child found comfort and touched into an inner presence that they never "learned" and that never left them.

Mother, a deer—that symbol of gentleness—just walked down my path as if to emphasize what you have said. The timing tells me this is a miracle, that nature is often the place of miracles, and that it offers the same to children.

Oh yes. Mother Nature raises her children in much the same way as an early and kind exposure to a loving Creator does. It can hardly be helped. Children are fashioned for wonder. To be religious is to be devoted to that which is of the utmost importance to you. Is it love? Is it fear? Is it wonder? So will your religion be.

But our way is also historical. As much as your culture believes in human history, religious history is often deprived of its place. In a society that dwells in facts, those facts that are discounted also speak volumes.

This is why we began, with Mirari, to return you to the wonder of this non-academic way. Memoria then drew you deeply into the realm of memory, expanding recollection of the past into remembrance of ways of knowing that are inclusive of the future. Metanoia now accompanies you into union with your subconscious, with your soul, and your soul unravels the ties that still bind you, freeing you "for," rather than "from," your time in eternity.

The soul and the feminine, like the imaginal, are metaphoric, slow, indefinite. Soul moves through and around experience and your reflections on your experience. None of it is instructional, nor can it be worked hard to attain. More importantly, our way can't be used. Can you imagine in your world a power that can't be used? As your Jesus said, "The power of being is the power to individuate the Self. The power to be who you are. This is power and the source of power. This is the force of creation, the only true power. But although each holds the power of creation, it is only in relationship that it is expressed and that we become powerful." [*]

---

[*] *ACOL* D:Day33.14-15, paraphrased

Use and Energy

What can *be used, in the way we're speaking of it, is associated with effort, solutions, study, work, and with accomplishments that are gained from efficiency and order.*

What comes of creativity, genius, and vision arises from expansiveness. Its association is one that moves and shares and communicates with empathy, creating the capacity for a sharing of feelings. You can see that these traits are present in both men and women, but more often overlooked by those men and women for whom a focus on practicality is what their training appears to demand.

The earthly presence of the masculine energy, whether in men or women, is such that it works hard to settle all matters quickly and definitively. Ideas not literalized are not often valued, because they can't be used. What "can" be used is prized and associated with solutions, with work, with gain and with profit.

When no longer confining their experience to practical uses, the gifts of masculine energy will experience a renaissance. Embracing their creativity freely, many will rise to protect this freedom for all, join the feminine and masculine within, and be present to offer all that their love of creation can provide.

The feminine realm we have moved into awaits many women as well. But don't get me wrong. "No use" does not mean one's actions are inconsequential. It is simply that in Metanoia's turn around, your process of conversion becomes your movement into spaciousness. It is crucial that what can't be used finds inclusion among the "doers," both masculine and feminine.

Use, in any form, leads to bondage, and so to perceive a world based on use is to see a world where freedom is impossible. What you think you need your sister for is thus based upon this insane premise that freedom can be purchased and that master is freer than slave. Although this is illusion, it is the illusion that is sought. The purchase price is usefulness. And so each joining is seen as a bartering in which you trade your usefulness for that of another. [. . .] From the simple concept of individuals needing to be in relationship to survive has grown this complex web of use and abuse.[*]

Now, we begin a gentler narrative of The New.

---

[*] *ACOL* C:9.43

CLOSING OUT THE OLD

FRAGILITY AND LACE

Mari, I want you and all your sisters and brothers of the feminine to know that fragility will lead to luminosity. Your fragile states reveal radiance from a single source: you . . . in the fullness of your union with Self and God. This state signifies a fertile interior relationship with conscious love.

There is a tenuousness about the fragile, as there is about The New. This binds them together. You might think you need bravery for The New but that's not the way it is. This isn't "solid reality" but vague reality, a single strand of one life's journey: a moment, a fragment of time. The arrival or departure of the tide. Fragility comes as a surge. Remember your book, Creation of the New, *and how it spoke of substantive truth:*

There is a field called the known truth, and it is what it is by agreement: there is a field of grass blowing in the wind.

There is also a field of substantive thought, a field of substantive feeling. There is a substantive field of spirit. There is substantive reality . . . or the unknown truth. . . . This substantive truth, and a reaching of this essential truth, as it is, in its actuality, is the experience that occurs with the faculty that has no name. It is the surprise. It is the unexplainable. It is the mystery, the unknown knowing. It is unquestionable.

These two fields of truth—that of agreement and that of substance—give reality to two worlds, two realms. Both are experienced as real. Those who discover the substantive truth, the unknown knowing, see these two worlds, some clearly, some obscurely. That they can be seen separately does not mean that they are separate in truth. The truth reveals one ultimate reality.*

This "substantive truth" is not the truth of facts agreed upon. Rather, it signifies direct knowing . . . remembered. In this case . . . remembered in Memoria for the revolution of Metanoia. Whether it is of a divine or human memory, or a current event, the fragile have noticed something that is of the feminine interior relationship with Self. It is often sparked by an exterior relationship with another and is like lacework over a paper pattern. Its intricacy causes the sense of fragility.

It can't be figured out. But the interior intricacy—revealed—shows the patterns. The entrenched patterns. One is often of doubt. Another is the unshakeable idea of needing to learn. Many have a deeply rooted penchant for giving without receiving or vice versa. All is revealed in the intricacy of the patterns! At just such a time as one simply can't stand back and view the lace, the time has arrived when she or he is accepting the new pattern. As you shared in A Course of Love, *the moment comes when you realize that you no longer have cause to fear your feelings. They are no longer the source of the misdirection of the past. This is a recognition that by being in the present you know your feelings are of the truth.†*

With this certainty that has no cause but seems to behave as an alternative to cause, you sense the coming picture of The New. Fragility is a sign that you are starting to accept who you are. These "given" feelings of the body reveal that of the old which are helpmates

---

* *Creation of the New*, p. 94

† *ACOL* D:Day8.21, paraphrased

to The New. The holding pattern is circumvented. The lace of fragility allows you to see-through the old pattern as it reveals what remains: the crucial mediating feelings. This is not mental interference. This is seeing that which is predominant and revelation of that which is latent.

The truth Jesus and I revealed was represented as a visual pattern that would aid understanding of the invisible. This is what you are now called to do. Whether you demonstrate the myth of duality or the truth of union, you are demonstrating the same thing. The way is to show your feelings, to make them visible. They are the creations unique to you.*

Seeing-through is a variation of pass through that relates to the act of incarnating. Incarnation is the miracle taking place in time. Seeing-through connects to what you can imagine in the view of your feelings and in the lace that overlays them. This is the intricate and beautiful web of The New. Here, with the tiny point of a needle, we begin to see the weaving together of truth and feelings. (There is no truth without feeling.)

Head bent, lacework in your hands, you see what is yours to keep and what is yours to let go. You see it is not as you imagined. As you create, you repattern. You see the human in a new divine light. Your fragile states will no longer feel threatening. They will feel beneficent. They are visitations.

---

* *ACOL* D:Day18.7 and 18.11, paraphrased

QUIETUDE

I get such a peaceful feeling from being alone. I don't even have to be in the cabin. Today I've been in the house, and there's been such a silence about it that I've almost been overwhelmed. The house is a good deal less noisy than the cabin. But at times she exceeds that, and I feel her wrap herself around me. Then each sound, the ticking of a clock, the creaks, the purrs of the furnace, seem filled with thirty years of familiarity. It is so peaceful.

In this tranquility I see that I've been knee deep in the fragile and nowhere near ready for the repatterning. If I formed the lace, I would only want to see through the hurt in an opaque way, not a way that would let it all pass through me and cleanse my consciousness of it. I realize I have not felt safe. Then the memories arise. I protect myself.

It's 8:00 now and I feel as if I've gotten off track and that there is no track. Just lace. And the lace is the pattern of our memories too, isn't it? We are bringing Mirari's wonder and Memoria's remembrance to our revolution of consciousness, aren't we? Bringing it all together.

Suddenly I feel it's possible, even probable, that "here" we encounter the other meaning of wonder. To let ourselves simply contemplate our lives—our hurts, our delicateness, as well as those places and situations where courage has found us and left us. To let amazement open the door to it all and reroute us into the beautiful lacework of The New. No matter how lonely, or painful, this is our crucible—the whole of it, bringing it all home. This is the end of the epidemic that has organized the chaos and managed the pain. This is the alchemy of changing form and the revolution of consciousness. Which is everything.

ℱULFILLMENT AND DESIRE

I have been held back by unfulfilled desire, haven't I Mary?

Yes, sweetie, you have. Any specific, but unfulfilled desire is a yearning for fullness of Self, even when that which needs to be recognized is still undiscovered. Now, with recognition come, you begin to feel your Self being freed of this concern.

Each one is tested and touched by the mercy of God—through their desires. There is no discrimination brought to bear on these marvelously different universes created by desire . . . there is only soul making.

Mary, I don't know how many have noticed, but Jesus spoke of desire almost five hundred times in *A Course of Love*. He called our "desire to be separate" the "most insane"[*] of the various desires we are caught up in. He didn't mean to banish desire but to draw forth true desire.

Tom Cheetham connected desire to Metanoia, saying:

It is by transformation of desire and not by its elimination that we live the revolution that is metanoia. The process of transformation is a process of ontological change. Unlike the being of a stone, for instance, human being admits of degrees. We can become more, or

---

[*] *ACOL* C:5.22

less, human. [...] We can become demonic or we can become holy—and everything in between.*

Don't you begin to wonder? To wonder what would happen if each one existed only in the glory of following the truth of their innermost desire? Would the dominator continue to be able to dominate? Or want to?

Now we look to possibilities that will create enough safety for the feminine ones to find and follow the potential that their desire reveals, for this embrace of potential is the first step to Metanoia's concluding liberation. Here we make an adjustment. We bring the spheres of our being into a true and effective relative position.

---

* Cheetham, Tom. *All the World an Icon*. Berkeley, North Atlantic Books, 2012, p. 246.

The New Orbit

Here, as you accept your birth into The New, you will enter a new orbit. Holy harmony is not found by staunch rigidity and will not be rectified by any notion that the female/male dynamic can remain the same. No. This dynamic change is very much about honoring the previously undervalued feminine. Fragility is needed to reveal the seams in the jewels and the repatterning of the light of vision to come—the vision of all true hearts—discovered through each one's wholeness. Those who are whole treasure union and do not seek to divide.

An orbit is a path. It will stay on track unless it is pushed or pulled beyond its capacity by the pressure of another system on its own. Having been pushed aside, the feminine is now on a new trajectory born in the brain and the heavens. This movement is no longer becoming, no longer latent. It is existent. The brain has been quiescent during this incubation period. Now this movement has developed. A response was stimulated. The new feminine orbit has been birthed.

Here, the feminine ones, female and male, residing in their own orbit, create a new cross of time and space. This movement of time is in tune with the clash of the divided sexes. It has come to be that this is part of the movement "to" the second coming. Before the coming together—the union and relationship that will create The New—the repatterning must commence. This will be, and remain, a fluid pattern that will allow the changes of The New.

It is through my assumption into Heaven, in form, that a new pattern of life was revealed. I, a "woman," was granted not only the gift of birthing the living holy one, but of rising to join Him. This was not a necessity and yet it was recorded. It remains important to this day as an example of women's power recognized. The power of body and soul rising together IS the revelation we see newly here.

As the feminine is released in each, she/he rises in your eyes. Your ears and your heart hear only one call, one voice, the language of one Source—that of the absolute equality of unity.*

This orbit is one that can represent the union, or wholeness, of Life as itself. Not human life alone. Not divine life alone. Not the life of the male or the female. Life as life. Not human life or divine life. Life. The unity of the human and divine Life—the incarnation of the soul within the flesh—the life now living Being.

No one can live "truly" outside of their own orbit just as no one can live with organs out of alignment. The organs within both male and female are laced together. So too are the feminine and masculine ways of being. Being laced together does not mean one or the other is obliterated. It does not mean that one can hurtle oneself into another's territory or derail another's orbit . . . not permanently. No.

Here, this new path allows the means for union and relationship of those who no longer appease the dominant.

Two, together—the duad—existing in harmony, is all that can halt the despoilers in this time. Orbital harmony is here and happening within. Here you accept that you have needs while ceasing to be needy or dependent. Here, you truly begin to see the fruits of giving and receiving as the joining of two in union.

This is metaphorical language for the duad of what you call "life on the ground" and the spacious self. The spacious self embraces all feelings.

---

* *ACOL* T2:4.19, paraphrased

LACE AND THE FEMININE

Waves, pulses and fields are the material means with which the subtle lace of the feminine is laid down with the care of the stars. "Lace" derives from a Latin word that speaks of an open space only outlined by thread. That open space is a good image for the inclusive feminine whose borders aren't dangerous or exclusive. Lace is delicate, lovely and tough. All passes through the lace into each one's particular form of movement, being, and expression . . . in unity and relationship. Knowing this is so, is what causes Metanoia, with no "effort." No effort "is" the revolution of consciousness. Outside of the strain of prescribed ways of knowing, the revolution simply happens.

This new and fluid pattern "of spacious form" was introduced in "The Dialogues:"

Now we listen to feelings.

Now we listen to feelings and understand what they have to say to us.

Now we listen with a new ear, the ear of the heart.

Now we recognize the thoughts that would censor our feelings, calling them selfish, uncaring, or judgmental. We examine. And we realize it is our thoughts and not our feelings that are selfish, uncaring, or judgmental. We realize this because we realize the sacred *space* we have become. Our space is the space of unity. It is the space of ease because thoughts are no longer allowed their rule.*

The Way of Mary will create and reflect the unity and relationship that has been just a breath away, withheld not for lack of willingness, but for lack of surrender to the unknown. The unknown is the spark to the flame, without which there is no fire.

The creation of this new pattern of consciousness is happening. It is "a happening" beyond your volition or control. It is underway in the new orbit. The imaginal serves your creatorship from a new location.

𝓜

But Mary, why the new orbit when we are hoping to unite? Even while I've always been drawn to spaciousness, I don't understand that. It's been the desire of my life to have room to breathe, to experience, to not have worries—which I know sounds like a desire to escape the human condition, but the human condition "in time" has become too complex. It really has. Ordinary things happen within ordinary days and my heart starts beating double time because, for some unknown reason, I'm confounded by the most regular of these cyclical human matters, such as paying bills. I've had that job all my life but passed it to Donny last year because he is willing to do it online. There are now only a few financial matters I need to tend to, yet they continue to draw up the same dread and discombobulation. Once I get started on them the whole day is ruined. Just thinking of it, my heart is pounding.

---

* *ACOL* D:Day12.1

And the same thing happens with less stressful areas of life if they suddenly become too noisy, or busy, or if a conflict emerges. I am so sensitive! I know this must be part of coming into The New and I hate to talk about it and discourage anyone, but I've got to be here for "me" too, Mary. I need you so much. My feelings at times can unmoor me. And we're about to speak of the spacious self, which I love the idea of, but I'm crying as I type this because I have become so "spacy" that my husband looks at me funny.

I give myself lots of leeway for doing this writing with you and Jesus, Mary, because I do know what it's like after three decades of experience. But there are new levels of intensity now. The atmosphere is different. It's never been easy to hold both worlds, or whatever you want to call it, but now... I'm just a mess. Not because of you but because I have to step back into the regular world and the shift of atmosphere that brings leaves my whole body feeling like it's cloudy, not just my mind. It's so hard to describe! But I'm floundering here.

And, since I've started in with this disclosure, I've got to tell you that I don't quite get the "new orbit." While I imagine you're talking of it as a way of embracing spaciousness, (which makes me practically salivate with a desire to somehow transcend this earthly reality without dying or running away), how does it bring unity?

There just seems no let-up. And if this is true for me, with a stable life and family, I can't imagine how stressful and terrifying everyday life is for anyone beginning to encounter The New, which to me IS spaciousness, within a busy or unstable life. This spaciousness makes hard reality almost unbearable.

Can you help me with that, please?

The orbit is metaphorical language for the duad of the spacious self, but apt. I want you, and all, to realize there are no boundaries here, and it's a perfect time to talk about it, because you so often wish for boundaries. You've been discovering this with such pain recently. To have no boundaries leaves you very susceptible to being disturbed by emotions, drama, bills, schedules, deadlines, shopping—all the normal and usual things of your time.

But what you see, what your eyes behold, what you hear in expressions, and in distortions of expressions of all kinds, is beginning to be so visible that your tender self can barely go on.

This is why I speak of the new orbit.

But how can this help me with life on level ground?

The idea, my daughter, sister, friend, is that you will have a new position from which to find, and share, spaciousness . . . even in the "here" of what you call "life on the ground." As we speak newly of the phenomenon of the universe, we include the universe of the body and within that body, the brain, which "lights up" much as do the heavens. It is this visual that I want you to imagine. The stars in the universe of your brain, and the sacred space they occupy.*

---

* See *ACOL* D:Day12.1: "...we realize the sacred space we have become..."

Taking a New Turn
THE BRAIN

We have given no mention yet to the brain, or much consideration regarding this personal universe. Since I know the brain may have little interest to you, we won't dwell on it, but I liken it to the priest who knows the rules and the priest who knows to "pray" the Mass. These are the potentialities of different and distinct phenomena, as of the yoke of rules or the free universe of the person and her heart.

What is going on within you now is a dialogue between the brain and the heart, and these two, the brain and heart, or we might say "mind and heart," are the home of much of creation's dialogue.

And so, you might ask, "What does this have to do with fragility?" I've brought this forward to form an image of the brain's lacework in an intricate and poetic manner. Its complexity rivals the blossom of the most elaborately bedecked flower, the twinkle of the heavenly stars. You have such lacework in you, too.

Your "own" lacework is both delicate and hardy, fragile and as mysterious and benign as the balance that is the universe itself. The universe is undivided. It might be said to have quadrants, but it is, itself, undivided multiplicity. So are you, and so are we, "together."

SHARING SPACIOUSNESS

All of time is included in the spacious self.

You, who were once passive co-creators of the pattern of consciousness that was learning in time, now become active creators of this consciousness that shares spaciousness in time outside of time. Doesn't this invigorate you?

The surrender that Metanoia inspires is the antidote to achievement. "Creation—which is of you and God in unity—will respond to your responses. Will respond to what you envision, imagine and desire. Creation of The New could not begin without you."* And you have been too pushed and pulled to begin... until now. Here, your presence in the new orbit will not be found by those who are not welcome to it. No one can hop onto your bumper or your train any longer. No one can push you off your balance.

I would love to surrender—feel I have surrendered *to you*—but I can't get myself to surrender to life as it was, and not only through lack of inclination. I am really floundering here. Yet at the same time I feel so close. Close to a very grand change.

Because you are! Here, you really can design anew. It's already happening in dozens of small ways that you've not discounted so much as failed to notice. This is very much like your worry about your health. You worry about your health because you are so different. You can't do all you used to do. Why might this be? Is your body really incapable? Or is it a lack of desire so strong that you can't force yourself? When change comes, do you imagine that it arrives without

---

* *ACOL* T4:12.34, paraphrased

these places in which you suddenly view yourself in a way you never have before? Where you see pain you previously dismissed? Where you become aware of options, even if you don't want to surrender to them?

Your greatest point of entry will be your true desire to yield the conscious mind to pass through from the imaginal realm. This pass through will be like the flashing in and out of new thought and memories as they are freed from "there" to "here." Coming unexpectedly, they may feel unwelcome, but you will come to embrace them as you have come to embrace us. They, too, are heaven sent. This design will assemble the "being" of the imaginal and reveal it to you in a way that will leave you undisturbed—an undisrupted unity.

You know you have experienced this already, and that is why you've been so drawn to the imaginal. You knew that, as a creative being, the imaginal would make you whole.

Wholeness is always and in all ways without ever being static. But it is only wholeness to you when you accept it. Wholeness comes in the swirl and the whirlwinds you are found to be ready for, the descending as well as the ascending, the masculine as well as the feminine, soul as well as heart. This is the way of the birth of the new babe, emerging whole and complete in the new time, the new unity . . . the new orbit. Taken out of what was to what will be, there is being . . . in relationship. Out of the darkness—light. Out of the fire of The New, with fragility and passion, the feminine will find increase for the birth of the new babe.

𝒯HE TWIN WHIRLWINDS AND THE INFINITY OF TIME

Mother, you've inspired me in such a way that this seems a good time to ask you about something that may take us in an expanded direction. It's about a vision that came to me in the evening, in a place from which I rarely look out: my sunroom office.

I remember that I heard popping sounds outside and raised the blinds to see what might be causing them. I wrote of it in *Mirari*.[*] I was on the phone with my friend Kate,[†] and described it then, saying "it was like we were twin vortexes of newness." But what stayed in my mind was that I'd "seen a vision of twin whirlwinds." For a few seconds they were moving toward me, but they quickly disappeared.

Then one day, about a year later, while I was online looking for something entirely unrelated, the image came to mind, and I typed in the words "twin whirlwinds." The first thing that popped up was a graphic that looked just like what I'd seen. I clicked on it, and found it was a sketch of feminine and masculine atoms! A little later, when the vision still wouldn't leave my mind, I purchased the book from which the image came. It is called *Occult Chemistry Illustrated Edition*, and was written in 1919 by Charles W. Leadbeater and Annie Besant. I saw right away that their "science" would go over my head, but I didn't mind the expense because there was the image I'd seen, preserved on paper. The authors wrote of the atoms:

---

[*] *Mirari*, p. 137

[†] Kate McNamara, psychotherapist and author of *Wholehearted Revolution, How One Woman Was Called Into Action*

In the one case force pours in from the "outside," from fourth-dimensional space, and passing through the atom, pours into the physical world. In the second, it pours in from the physical world, and out through the atom into the "outside" again, i.e., vanishes from the physical world. The one is like a spring, from which water bubbles out; the other is like a hole, into which water disappears. We call the atoms from which forces come out positive or male; those through which it disappears, negative or female. All atoms, so far as observed, are of one or the other of these two forms.

The atom can scarcely be said to be a "thing," though it is the material out of which all things physical are composed. It is formed by the flow of the life-force and vanishes with its ebb. When this force arises in "space"—the apparent void which must be filled with substance of some kind, of inconceivable tenuity—atoms appear; if this be artificially stopped for a single atom, the atom disappears; there is nothing left. Presumably, were that flow checked but for an instant, the whole physical world would vanish, as a cloud melts away in the empyrean. It is only the persistence of that flow which maintains the physical basis of the universe.[*]

The word "tenuity" reminds me of how I have, at times, called my own reality tenuous, without ever having looked at its meaning: a thinning of the veil! I bring that up because I don't understand the science.

Yet this is one of the most bizarre, and also wonderful findings I've had when exploring visions that have come to me. Most intriguing is its relationship to the feminine and masculine about which we've been

---

[*] Besant, Annie, and Leadbetter, Charles. *Occult Chemistry Illustrated Edition*, CreateSpace Publishing, 2011, pp. 22-23.

writing. It speaks to me of possibly existing "in" and even "as" the unity and distinction that is both supporting and being supported by the cosmos, which all together is pure possibility, the All of Everything that is God.

I wonder if our atoms could provide for our intimate recognition of unity and distinction rather than opposites and contradiction.

Let's take your idea even farther than that.

*Jesus described "the body as the dot in the wider circle" and asked you to "accept that your discovery of your natural talent or ability and your discovery of new ideas are discoveries of something that already existed beyond the dot of the body." He then said that "[I]f you accept that these ideas that already exist were able to pass through you in order to gain expression in form; then you are beginning to see, on a small scale, the action that, on a large scale, will become the new way."** See this along with your discovery of the flow of atoms that pour "into" the physical world and that pour out "through" the physical world.*

He wanted you to see form as a way for the eternal to join with you here and now.†

You can't start too big, my daughter. This is why Jesus spoke of a territory of shared consciousness, saying that it "exists within the larger consciousness of unity, just as the territory of your body exists within the larger territory of the planet Earth. We will begin here . . . knowing that discovery and revelation will expand this territory and realizing that no matter how small this cosmic sphere may be, it will still at times give way to awareness of the All of Everything."‡

---

* *ACOL* D:9.14, paraphrased

† See *ACOL* D:9.13

‡ *ACOL* D:7.29

Jesus then took us from the All of Everything to the particular, asking us to concentrate on a simple idea: that each of us contains a natural ability or talent that existed prior to the time of learning.* This worked so well for me! It's how I feel about writing, and I'm sure that this is where my awareness of the All of Everything arises and expands. And I have to say, Mary, how much I love being surprised when the way in which we begin the day takes me somewhere totally unexpected.

These ideas have reminded me of how, through the extension of our being into union, we complete a circuit, a circle of giving and receiving as one, and cause and effect are complete.† This simpler language is easier on me than science, Mary.

But you did get me intrigued enough to investigate a little and I found (on Wikipedia) that Baruch Spinoza seemed to say something very similar, and he uses the word "attribute," which you don't hear often, and yet Jesus said it over 50 times in *ACOL*, including in variations such as "attribute-laden" and "attributeless."

Baruch Spinoza defined God as "a substance consisting of infinite attributes, each of which expresses eternal and infinite essence," and since "no cause or reason" can prevent such a being from existing, it therefore must exist. This is a form of the ontological argument, which is claimed to prove the existence of God, but Spinoza went further in stating that it showed that only God exists. Accordingly, he stated that "Whatever is, is in God, and nothing can exist or be conceived without God." This means that God is identical with the universe, an idea which he encapsulated in

---

* See *ACOL* D:8.3 and D8.10

† *ACOL* D:Day40.1, paraphrased

the phrase "*Deus sive Natura*" ('God or Nature') [...] God can be known by humans either through the attribute of extension or the attribute of thought. Thought and extension represent giving complete accounts of the world in mental or physical terms. To this end, he says that "the mind and the body are one and the same thing, which is conceived now under the attribute of thought, now under the attribute of extension."

After stating his proof for God's existence, Spinoza addresses who "God" is. Spinoza believed that God is "the sum of the natural and physical laws of the universe and certainly not an individual entity or creator." Spinoza attempts to prove that God is just the substance of the universe by first stating that substances do not share attributes or essences and then demonstrating that God is a "substance" with an infinite number of attributes, thus the attributes possessed by any other substances must also be possessed by God. [...] God is the only substance in the universe, and everything is a part of God.[*]

Even though I don't feel that I understand fully, I've gone on and on with this, Mother. It intrigued me for a reason.

This is a wonderful exploration that can bring us back to your Jesus' words of extension, and the completion of a circuit, a circle of wholeness,[†] which is happening now with the feminine and masculine of being. This was also heralded by your twin whirlwinds.

In our time, certain people were called "heralds" and were messengers and envoys. You see in much the way they did. Not

---

[*] "Baruch Spinoza." *Wikipedia.* https://en.wikipedia.org/wiki/Baruch_Spinoza. Accessed February 10, 2024.

[†] *ACOL* D:Day40.1

everyone saw. And not many of those who saw paid attention. But the Eastern Magi were what you now call astrologers, and the apostle Matthew what you might call a natural historian and biographer. They took notice. All who track changes with eyes open to the heart, reveal that it beats out the rhythm of time. Each one's time.

Life, history, astrology . . . everything is a flow . . . as are the atoms of the feminine and masculine. You do not need to know the science my daughter. You are more like Matthew than the Magi. But you are doing just what those of my time did. None of us "knew for sure" from these heralds of our day unless we felt it in our being. We didn't always know right away, and we seldom knew "what" we knew. Do you see? This is what faith is and what faith fills in for us over time. "Your time," this time, is another period like ours when faith in oneself and one's knowing is "the way."

Whirlwinds symbolize God's overwhelming presence as an unstoppable, unalterable force. You don't have to try so hard to understand.

Thank you, Mother! I do feel that faith fills-in the "gaps" for me, and very simply. I feel that You, as the feminine creator of life, are also an expression of an undivided movement to "become" that flow once again, with none greater, and none lesser.

WHOLEHEARTED FREEDOM

I know the word "wholehearted" is not being used only to convey "head and heart" or "heart and brain" or "thought and love." It's about wholeness first, and so also about finding freedom from the conflict that divisions spark. It's the very liberation from external authority that Metanoia instigates. Wholeheartedness allows us to be unreservedly devoted and sincere toward ourselves and our givens. It is from this that the true extension of soul—that which "is" the given—moves the heart to heal into being. Our givens are our uniqueness.

I wrote of this twenty years ago in my little book, *The Given Self*:

There's a Cause with a capital C that feels like it holds the givens you can't abandon, even if you want to, and causes with a little 'c' that pull you away from them. There are influences that you hold close and others you can't abide so that you've got this shoring up and shedding going on at the same time. All I can really tell you is that there are things that don't feel right for reasons you mainly don't understand, and things that do for reasons equally obscure.[*]

You were admitting to knowing then what I'm saying now. There, in each soul's givens, is where one's feeling-toned words arise, and brilliance shines.

---

[*] *The Given Self*, p. 30

WHOLENESS

Your vision reveals that many will, in this time, bear the truth of feminine and masculine wholeness as I once did. In this orbital balance, the new form of wholeness will come to Earth. Here, the Divine Mother in each is invited to hold this God-giving life within. United in wholeness, the masculine and feminine are honored and welcomed to give birth—to bring forth new life—again. To bring forward the second coming.

My Mother love has come to the birthers of The New and has provided a place apart from those who have pushed and pulled away from gestation and brought life near to the point of destruction. You are here to birth despite the disregard of those who are too blind to see what they destroy. To spin past those who refuse to realize what they do. This new balance has come to allow for free movement, being and expression in the orbital plane.

You will spend a while now, feeling out your new freedom, and pushing the edges of your body's allegiance to you. Invite your body fully into this experience, of universal Christ Consciousness, where it can be a welcome partner in this new beginning. We are bringing the truth of the revolution to life, as all that you have seen as "parts of the self, such as male and female, conception and action, inspiration and manifestation, are brought together in spaciousness."*

In your case, and that of many women, it is an invitation to release yourselves from self-protection and to engage with tenderness. I remind you that the time of tenderness is the release of bitterness.

---

* *ACOL* T1:8.17, paraphrased

Bitterness and uncertainty are replaced by hope. Hope is the condition of the initiate, new to the realization of having a home within the embrace.*

Self-protection, which you are intimately familiar with, is often a form of fear, but is warranted in times when you are fearful for cause. You experienced causes for self-preservation many times in life: from physical attacks, to living in poverty, to acting as protector of your children and grandchildren. You rose above timidity to protect your Course of Love *from the rigidity of learning, and its "one right way" answers. I've waited until now to bring this up because, like so many changes of Metanoia, the higher mind (a Greek definition of Metanoia, with "meta" meaning above and Nous meaning mind) that rises above, is different now.*

In The New, the above and the below are undivided.

---

* *ACOL* C:20.36

Surrendering
to the Current of the New

What makes Metanoia's revolution so different, and so revolutionary, is the surrender at the end of the seeking. That to which you surrender now is not that of the past. Today's surrender is to new knowing. You surrender to the current of The New.

As unusual as it sounds, a significant part of The New is giving up choices. Seeing what is there. Seeing what is there for what it is. "Surrender" is the last thing we ever want to do, and yet it moves us beyond what can be urged.

It sounds benign but surrender remains the great change agent it has always been . . . when it is surrender to the truth of your experience.

Yes! It calls forth what "each" of us desires most, according to our individual natures. "Eachness replaces thingness" even when we don't know it.

When you're not deciding, you can know. That's the revolution! It's a revolution because when you know, there is no following. Learning ends. The New begins to well up and issue forth.

With Metanoia I have given myself over to knowing newly and do my best to allow what doesn't come as much as what does.

Here you invite the eternal that resides in your subconscious knowing, in your soul's yearning, in your dreams, and in creation of The New.

I now know self-surrender evokes the eternal nature of miracles. I surrender to Mirari's wonder, and the expanded remembrance of Memoria, and feel secure in knowing that with the great turning of

Metanoia, the imperative is to know Self "first." To not tamp Self down but to become intimate with Self.

I understand this "with you" and by way of my intimacy with my surrounds. I am in union *here*. I know my Self and my plot of ground *here*. And I've come to truly know a few people too, in unity and relationship, as they've come to know me in the *here* in which we abide.

Here, in surrender, we know the deep mystery of *each other*, and see it as the grace of this life. And I love that it comes of knowing ourselves as other than we are in separation. That's what invites vulnerable sharing and allows knowing and being known . . . which is everything.

I can see incarnation as an enactment, an embodiment, and an embrace of the imaginal in time's new cycle. It is of what can be imagined being made real as each soul leads the way.

We really are birthing The New. We are doing this in truth.

We are doing this in time.

We are birthing the children of The New. You.

You are precious ones come.

Now we envision each new babe birthing into the world, coming in with the feminine as primary. Just a touch ahead of the masculine so to balance the duad, as all is about creating the new configuration, a wholeness that is ever evolving.

I am back to the rock and rocking very strongly.

You are holding yourself . . . rocking the new babe who is you. **Metanoia is the birthing revolution, making all things new.** Remember, "all are capable of birthing the Self."*

---

* *ACOL* T1:9.7

Your own new lives are what you are birthing. You are pregnant with the coming of your own true Self. You are coming to life, and your new lives will create The New.*

---

* *Memoria*, p. 44

Flashes

One day my Hawk speaks to me, conveying the words: "Don't doubt what you do here."

I say, "Okay."

Then I hear, "Trust your vantage point."

I see the hawk's feathers ruffle though there is no breeze and imagine him preening. The stillness is complete except for me and the hawk who has claimed me.

Then I hear, "The laws of gravity may change."

The endless dried twigs of winter, on the limbs of at least seven trees, hold my messenger of The New. Each time I move my head he is in a smaller triangle. Triangle upon triangle.

The telescope vision that comes to me occasionally blinks on. It flashes on and off, like the flashing in and out of new knowing. Remembering it, I think, "Oh my God, it *is* the same thing, isn't it?" It's probably there throughout recorded history. Some way of describing these rushing visions, these glimpses of another realm, the animal kingdom, or the eternal beyond. They come like the hawk's own movements—so fast you can't actually "see" them.

I find myself crouching over the table. My feet are on the meditation kneeler, my knees just under the table lip. I am in the position of the women at the campfire, in view of the clearing that once became their circle of fire. I lean in further to see the hawk, my elbows on my knees. I clasp my hands together and they rest over my heart. All naturally. My toes start to create a rocking motion. I only notice this after the fact.

Another hawk wings past. It has begun.

Time Outside of Time Is Finding Us

"Creation of The New takes place in time outside of time," Mary says.

Truth and illusion are both present in time. "In time," belief in the semblance of reality is a continual occurrence, bringing about your questionable leaders, your tyrants, your disparity of wealth and poverty, your racial clashes, and your brutality of the strong inflicted upon the weak, as of men upon women.

Sometimes, the illusion of reality has to become so evident, so glaring, its acceptance so unacceptable, its difference from truth so clear—that the spark to a great movement begins.

They will say, "I did not know!" with great dismay.

I certainly don't know of this in the way you do, Mary, but I have felt time changing. So have many of the women, and a few of the men I speak to. Something is different "in us" that is making time different. I trust that we—body, mind, heart, soul—are in every way "in" the transition to time outside of time as we've known it.

Yes, Mari. This is true, and it is not a season for you, or your sisters and brothers, to be timid or meek. It is the occasion for you to pick up your mantle for the dawn of this transition.

I know that we need to support each other and do so with eyes wide open to the truth . . . and to the false. But mainly to The New. We have been prepared for it.

What is the Transition?
Surrender to the New

As Jesus predicted over twenty years ago, you have been made ready for the fulfillment of the way of Jesus and the inception of our way— the way of the Marys.

You have been preparing for this final stage of the fulfillment of the way of Jesus. You have also been preparing for the beginning of the fulfillment of the way of Mary. Many of you will follow the way of Jesus to completion, beginning a stage of interaction with the world, an interaction with the miracles that will aid in the dismantling of the old and with preparing the way for the birth of the new. Others of you will follow your hearts to a bypassing of the final stage of the old and to anchoring [T]he [N]ew within the web of reality.*

Jesus spoke of "creating [T]he [N]ew by means other than doing,"† and noted this is a new way for us.

Mary, these aren't isolated things happening, are they? The events, the tears, and the expressions of courage, they're related somehow. As are our areas of focus here. Aren't they a chance for a new beginning? A chance for rejection of the old, of the lies, of those who would distort truth and our memory of what is truly real. I'm speaking of this because of memory's link to whatever this is that is transpiring within me, and within time and space. Because

---

* *ACOL* D:Day18.1
† *ACOL* D:Day19.13

sometimes my memory fails me so completely that I feel like I'm losing my mind.

I read something recently about the way memory responds to assault, and I know it is true. I have only snippets of memory from my two attacks. Our brains work in a way that is protective of us, allowing us to remember selectively, but by that, I don't mean by choice.

I know there are explicit and implicit ways of remembering. With the implicit you can't "retrieve" the memory at will.

My surmise is that whatever is happening now is like these ways of memory. What we're speaking of, if I'm getting it at all, feels so like that! The knowing is there within, but not retrievable. The truth is there but not as a set of facts to be drawn up. The unknown knowing is obscured until the memory of it is cued by something. When I forget, in "regular life" situations, I feel out of control. But in this "new" life, I am (mostly) calm within this "unknown knowing." It feels innately part of me. I lose both the sense of knowing and of forgetting.

As I was typing, the word "cued" flashed at me, and I see again that it is in this way, with cues and clues, with the implicit rather than the explicit, that The New is finding us, reminding us, and even warning us.

You have already surrendered to The New. This is your acknowledgment of that. But you are still growing into the simultaneous experience that reveals the wholeness of time.

In the new turning, everything comes to you with an innocence of intent.*

---

* *Memoria,* p. 384

"Time outside of time" by itself will not cause the shift that needs to occur. ...What will create the shift is the ability to experience "time outside of time" and "time" simultaneously. Thus is the "wholeness" of time, or eternity, experienced and made real. Eternity might thus be seen as the unchanging constant that has not been affected by the variable of time. Said in another way, eternity and time are part of the same continuum as are properties such as hot and cold. They are part of the same whole that is the constant of all that is whole—all that is one.[*]

---

[*] *ACOL* D:Day28.20

Like the Moon

Good morning my Holy Ones,

The moon is now, in the last minute of this day's sixth hour, almost totally obscured by clouds. If I didn't know it was there, I would be wondering what that stroke of lightness in the sky was—not what it hid. The hidden.

My glasses were off. Now, with them on, there's a fraction of the crescent like a bright claw in the sky. The top of the crescent is the visible part, though it passes in and out of sight. At 6:02 it is invisible. At 6:03 it has reappeared. What a dance! Now at 6:05 there is a moonbeam, vertical rather than horizontal, but still, knowing the moon is there, I know it is a moonbeam.

My mother, I am not yet brave and bold. I am like that moon. Peeking out. Going back undercover. There are blocks and resistances, and denial. The need for courage. You just don't know you've got the blocks and resistances until you do—just like you don't realize you've gone full circle and are standing somewhere new, in some different place, that place as new as are you.

You find yourself again. Peeking in and out of the high places from your spot before the window.

ℬEING TRULY CHOICELESS

"My Holy Mary," I say, "I know I am not done changing but I am DONE with the old." I know this, not only because I can't do it anymore, but because I do not *want* to do it anymore, and I know I don't have to define what that means. I know it because I feel it.

I was talking to my son, Ian, one night, of "what's been happening lately"—in a perfectly ordinary conversation—when it *came over me* that I have been demonstrating that *I am done*, in a personal way, with several situations that had been of concern. I was demonstrating this without having a conscious realization of what it was I was doing. And I wasn't thinking of any "of this" at all when I told him, in that casual conversational way, that the manner in which I'd acted newly wasn't based on a decision I'd made. "I just *knew*," I said.

You're starting, my Mari, to be released from the confines of your logical, practical mind.

Yes! I don't even need to ask the question, but I'll ask it anyway. Is it my subconscious mind that knows in this new way? With this choicelessness? Because, Mary, I've noticed other situations, other times of choice, in which I'd already had that same choiceless feeling. There was nothing to "decide" because I already "knew." Something had shifted. Within this dialogue, something has really shifted in me.

I have begun to be ... unconscious. That is the only way I can think to put it. **I have no, or very little, consciousness of my old knowing. I am only conscious of what I know as I know it. But ... now I know I love myself ... more.** And I'm rocking like crazy.

I can feel that I am no longer a border to myself, but I do have a border when needed. Both feelings are New.

The psychological words are just words to me, but I'm more in touch than ever with what's given me inspiration, intuition, creativity, and inner knowing. I think of what I have with you and Jesus as a spiritual blessing that is "felt," but I'm thankful for this new understanding. I've needed to understand this, so I don't feel like I'm losing my mind!

It's refreshing to just know, to not have any qualms. You used the word refreshing once, Mother, saying, "We, of the way of the Marys, are refreshing that which has grown stale, that which thinks it knows what to do, that which clings to the way it has been done..."[*] It fits so perfectly! That's exactly what this feels like and what we've spoken of as shared knowing.

Shared knowing is very akin to what the Buddhists call interbeing and interdependent origination. In the simplest of ways, in an effortless conversation, you realized something that you've avoided realizing for a long time. It came naturally when you were ready. This IS the way! Your Jesus gave you a clue when he spoke of the "web of reality,"[†] which is about limitless connections, all of which have significance and implications. He didn't ask you to track these connections but said one way is active and one way is receptive. This is like a network of acts and encounters, masculine and feminine, that can alter your path in a cause-and-effect manner.

Yes, Mary, thank you for reminding me. It was Day 18 when Jesus said that some of us would follow our hearts "to a bypassing of the final stage of the old and to anchoring the new within the web of

---

[*] *Mirari*, p. 321

[†] see *ACOL*, Dialogues, Days 18 and 19

reality." And you and I, Mary, began our way of Mary with women anchoring The New!

Non-Linear Time

Morning! The sense of something "really and truly" happening with time is observable at this early hour. No wonder I love it so.

"Here," I'm letting the dark-turning-blue of this beautiful horizon affect me, and I am content. As long as it's not yet light, and I get my time in the dark and the quiet, I can let every mystery of the universe be unraveled by our dialogue's composition.

I feel you near, Jesus, and am so aware that there is no straight line, my Brother. It's more like an undeviating existence through constant renewal . . . or relationship. Maybe the shift that needs to occur can't happen without relationship!

I am allowing the possibility that the "swirls" of time have found me. That I am beginning, through the life of my soul, to hold and be held by the swirls of time!

It feels natural to me that, as I "plot out" anything, I see it within the line of time. My bread takes twenty minutes to bake and that is the way of time. It goes from here to there in a straight line. And in this case, there are "results" that occur due to the time of baking. I've forgotten time and ruined the bread far more often than I care to say! I do have to carry on in time. The way we humans think of all "doing" is like baking bread. It is occurring "in time" . . . everything, máybe, other than creating.

The thing about creating outside of time/in time is that it's like being in two places at once. Being multi-spatial! When I'm creating and the bread dough rises out of the pan, forgotten, it's because when I'm inspired, linear time gets away from me. I've been released from time internally even though it continues to be my external reality. I'm in an alternate time zone, "gone" from ordinary time. Especially when I'm with you, my Holy Ones, but not only then. I've seen that if my writing isn't creative in the way that takes me out of time, I won't like the result. I will hear it and feel it in the words. They may look fine and form complete sentences, but they will be absent that little "something extra" that transforms clock-time's linearity.

M

I'm settling down now, and being here, really "here." I know I'm not ever strictly on my own. Thank you, Jesus, and I thank you, Mary, for this dialogue that has granted me a greater sense of Twoness: two together as one, as I wrote in *Creation of the New*.

The great birth is the birth of oneness into twoness, the explosion of a new creation where union to union, all to all, there is relation.[*]

> *Our dialogue is always of the two, even when you can't see it "here." We are the two in union, composing a narrative of The New. We do this through the duad of inspiration and willingness, you and me, Jesus and you . . . in dialogue.*

I do see it here, and it's not as jarring as I thought it would be. I am ready. And I say that as, in the blink of an eye, the horizon flashes into day, flooding the path outside my window with light.

---

[*] *Creation of the New*, p. 85

The Sabbatical

It's evening of the first day of my husband Donny's annual trip and I find myself in familiar territory. This time has come to feel like the true start of my year, the interior part.

I'm alone, watching the night sky lighten in a way that makes no sense. It's glowing brightly, just like morning, and there's a more insubstantial hue to the horizon than there was when I sat down. Such an amazing and peculiar world, even when nothing appears to move in the slightest degree. It's an incredibly calm night. But I admit I don't have my glasses on. That could be part of it.

I don't necessarily mean to start a big conversation but there is something about being in the house by myself. Being ... alone. Knowing no one is coming home. Knowing I will have days to myself. There is not one thing going on tomorrow. Just me and this beautiful time of hunkering down quietly with you, Mary.

Yesterday, Lee shared with me that Jesus once said something to Helen like ... "stay sharp." I told him I thought you were asking me to stand up more boldly. He said, "Instead of being who you are?"

Isn't that interesting!

It's true that I don't want to do much but be here. I don't believe I want to be a voice "in the world" outside my doors—at least not in ways other than this. I'm plenty bold right here. I need time without pressure, which I really haven't gotten yet, despite the hours I spend doing mindless things. Those things, too, are my antidote to the enormity of what we're talking about.

Looking out the window, this whole experience feels like a metaphor for seeing and not seeing. It is the very murkiness of the dark that is revealing. The light can, at times, be too obvious. It is not the same day in Australia that it is here. Kate, on her side of the world, is nearly at midday. Our planet spins. We are living in a very different time, and in many different times that we call "zones." And we can "connect" even so.

Long, slow work occurred to discover the spin of the world. In your time, Mary, the world was seen as flat. Heaven was a city above the clouds. And whatever greater knowledge of this was held by Jesus or the Magi, this was still the belief until... Galileo. How could the world today not be different? It's a different world even from when Helen Schucman lived. Vastly different. I'm so glad you speak of prophecy being particular to time and place. Some things are the same almost everywhere: spoons and knives, fences and bicycles. But not time. Not day and night.

How different will it be in 30 more years? Are we in the end-stage that climate change suggests? No single event to blow up the world but a thousand candles to wicks lighting off plagues and floods and wars? Pestilence. The old Biblical prophecies coming to visit again. Predicted again, only this time by scientists—scientists who have gotten us well into the plague of our own knowledge, and the wonders of it, too. Heaven and hell, together. The dark and the light. The advance and the consequence. The before and the still to come. The swirling vortexes of time.

And yet this hope, this faith, this gallant movement of the poets of the inner life, lives on, and we, with our designs on unraveling the queendom within, carry it into being.

I see more clearly now, and to not acknowledge this would be a mistake. I have, I feel a certain "heavier wisdom" and a "lighter heart." I'm not sure what kind of combination that is. I say this as I look out once again, on a night scene hardly different from the morning scene I view each day, but not a replica either.

That's almost exactly the kind of thing that happens "here," that thing I'm trying to describe. It's that subtle. Take a photo, this time of year, at 6 pm or 6 am and you'd be hard pressed to know if it was a view of day or night. That's how tricky this "holiness" is in some way.

My belated New Year "review" makes me wonder if I have any choice over the way that is mine. I see and feel my changes, my "maturity," constantly now. It's very different. I am different. I've been honed, I could say, by my life struggles and by *A Course of Love*. I have unlearned some old ways of doing things, with Jesus and with you, Mary. But sometimes I struggle *more* due to that unlearning . . . because so much, if not everything, is of The New.

The Cross of Time and Space

Sitting quietly at the dining room table, I look out and see a *cross* on the window of the cabin. Slender. The horizontal line a tad high. Simple, white. It remains as I move about to gauge the line of light. I remember the "cross of time and space."

This is . . . unexpected. It feels "heavy" and instantly affects me at a very deep level. I feel Jesus with me, and say, "I accept everything you want to bring before me." In turn, he says, **"[H]ere is what we will do with suffering. We will take it away once and for all. We will crucify it on the *cross of time and space*, bury it, so that it need be no more, and demonstrate that new life follows the choice to end suffering."**[*]

"Sister," he continues, "While I was not birthed 'so that' I could be crucified, I did allow it to happen in the sense of not choosing to prevent what was occurring. I remained within the wisdom of God and knew that pain and suffering were what the people of the time understood 'as the way to change'—which you still do as well, you and many sisters and brothers of the physical realm. But aren't you ready now for greater understanding of 'the cross of time and space?'"

"I hope so," I say.

"The cross of time and space is what you are standing 'in and within,' as you say. See the place, in the reflection before you, where the lines of the cross join. This is the dot in the circle, representing the monistic nature of the unified whole, or field of reality.

---

[*] *ACOL* D:Day2.23, emphasis added

"And you might call it the collision of the realms.

"Do you realize how fervently this clash of the realms has been represented throughout time and into your present day? The imagination runs wild with epic versions, one after another, of the collision of time and space! It is 'in the collective consciousness.' There is a knowing.

"We are one-ing the universe, inviting Earth to be imagined back into the spacious harmony of the heavens where it has always resided. We are preparing the safe passage in which you can experience this new time and allow it to exist in your reality of consciousness. This, too, is the revolution of Metanoia. It is another aspect of what your twin vortexes demonstrate—the reality of your consciousness coming to awareness of how vastly you are connected to the cosmos and to the power to 'allow' time to change, to allow time to come into you. In your universe of one is the universe of the many. You said it yourself: You believe you have the power to change the world. You do."

"Dear Brother," I say, "I know this human journey is so damn beautiful and peculiar and heart breaking. And you know what, Jesus? This isn't suffering to me. This is *honoring*. Remembering."

"My sister, now you might say, 'Remember me when you come into The New, this celestial womb of The New.' Memory is binding and beautiful and I bless your tears that fall again. Memory connects all time and all space. All pain and all love. Are you ready to see this?"

I'm rocking and crying like crazy. I tell Jesus, "I feel that I truly could cry a flood."

"You have now," Jesus says, "a population large enough and wholehearted enough, to redeem all compassionate being of all time. You redeem those who did not know as you redeem yourself.

You change the future by changing the past and change the past by changing the future. I leave you to it with a hint to revisit Day 37."

One of the reasons you have been as intent as you have been on your idea of a separate and particular God is that you want to believe that there is a compassionate being in charge of everything, looking out for you, there to help when you are in need. God is all compassionate being everywhere—not one being of compassion! In union and relationship you realize this. And you realize that all compassionate being everywhere is a consciousness or beingness that you share. And further, you realize that what is possible is for you to become the one being of compassion that you already are in God . . . You realize that the call for the second coming of Christ has sounded and that it is a call to the difference you have always desired while not requiring you to remain separate!*

---

* *ACOL* D:Day37.9-10

Ensoulment of the World

With "your" ensoulment of "your world," all realms become protectorates, listening for your heartbeat in that dominion which will find its completion in you. You, and the heartbeat of "your" world, are synonymous with "the world."

The world extends itself into each element of being as you step out of the way of your thinking mind. You might say it's time to "get out of the way" of time so that it can unfold and enfold you in the embrace of Love.

The Dynamic

The dynamic of The New asks you to know nothing, to dwell in astonishment.

Realize that what your friend Rev. Rhetta Morgan called the "magnet" of Mother energy is what is drawing you. The magnet of Mother energy is bringing the eternity of Christed reality to time through its natural origins: what you call magnetic fields in the universe. They are a force of continual change, rather than what you might think of as the unchanging.

The emboldened feminine is rising for the gain of both men and women. This is a poignant time that is neither sad nor distressing. It is, rather, a time of uplifting, happening with great care.

Here, we are in view of the vibrant and forceful landscape of the miracle enacted in time and space.

The Power to Imagine

Metanoia is the miracle of the turnabout, an actual revolution of time and space. With it, humanity is facing a new partnership with Heaven so as to see and know newly. You evolve from the endless cycle of misfortune into a new cycle of opportunity. Let's say it is an "opportune" time, dear heart. This is another word with wonderful associations that have nothing to do with getting rich! The opportune is heading to a safe harbor and suggests doing so at the appropriate time.

It is the appropriate time for the creation of The New and the widening of our emotional depth. I know this, and that they go together.

Every soul has a destiny, which you could also call a vocation, one of rediscovering all that has been exiled.

Rediscovery comes of unitary, wholehearted thought, led by inspiration. Yes, we are bringing your attention to thought again, which doesn't mean "thinking." It is your "thought" that becomes inspired by the "incoming" of The New: the wholehearted thought that is of the melding of mind and heart. With mind and heart's unity regained, thought can once again be about conception and the power to imagine.

Everything now is of the co-mingling two that, in Creation of the New,[*] *you called "twoness." It's now revealing a new third: two in union with creation.*

---

[*] *Creation of the New*, p. 85

Since the start of this pandemic, people around the world have come into a period of intense longing. They are now ready to welcome the soft residence within, which has about it the blending, melding energy of The New, energy that covertly reveals new life to you, as you. Your Brother and I are with you and all people.

Despite the heartache and death, please see that your movement need not be delayed. Right in the midst of this great disruption of what was, the harmony of the heavens will come together in each of you and in the joining of you. Each who leave Earth, and each who remain.

Here, we continue to unify Heaven and Earth: female and male, body and soul—all that have only appeared to be divided. Sovereigns unite in the new orbit inspired by conception and action, inspiration and manifestation. You will create the union of the realms and a time of miracles.

We, of the heavens, watch over the babe of The New: Love Incarnate. You. This is the wholeness of love given to love along with the almighty stamina that will bear the process.

Fragility

Mary, I know I have covered over my tenderness with protection, and I hope to cease doing so. Tenderness is what you and Jesus invited me to, and I am here to atone for not getting it. Yes, I am here to atone. This is my atonement, each and every morning, for all I do and don't do. I feel kind of lousy and not proud of myself today, and compassion for myself, and my daughters.

It's an exquisite, deep black morning that just took that double turn in which it appears suddenly darker and at the same time a hint of blue rises. There's a bright star—three stars, actually, with one brighter than the others in a quite brilliant way. Donny fed the animals, and a bunny is out. Yesterday was a rough one. It was 14 below in the morning.

The fragility.

I'm beginning to long for the time when it won't be so bare that the streetlights, unseen in other seasons, find their way into my woods. They're shining where the freeway's exit ramp meets the neighborhood street. What an assault they are. Noise. Bright colors. Discord. Not feeling proud of myself. In the blaze of brake lights, the exhaust from a stopped car turns red and rises above the fence into my view like scarlet smoke.

I am a problem to myself.

Yes, at the moment you are. Do you want release?

Actually, yes. (I almost said no.)

I know.

I've turned my position now, so that when I sit back I can't see the lights.

Shadows have laid themselves down across the strait of snow, revealing such a lovely variety of shapes: crisscrossed lines illuminating XX's and triangles and train tracks.

Thank you, Lord and Mother, for everything, and for every release of the mood I've got in me.

M

And then ...

Oh, Lord and Mother. Suddenly, I'm full to bursting, like I have a ten-pound baby in me, waiting to be birthed.

Why wouldn't you be aching for your own birth? One that is offering you freedom.

Oh, I have such a feeling that this is what is happening, in me, and every woman friend I have.

Now a big ol' crow has appeared.

The crow is alert and warns you of dangers. This crow has been your companion a long while and will be with you while you adjust to the birthing revolution of The New.

Darkness and light are becoming opaque, flexible, no longer a tag team but mutable. And the words are back in a manner that is no longer so direct as to obscure the mystery. Oh, my God, just true words as the expression of the soul! What more is needed?

I remain in the dimly lit and the dimming of the noise . . . .

A TRIBE OF PERSONIFIED BEING

You and I, Mari, have composed a cosmology of life in Love. We dwell in the space-time relationships of the cosmos and speak of revolution in the manner of a new tribe of personified being. We give voice to the mystery that envelops us "all." And "all" is "all." No one is "going to hell in a handbasket," as your elders used to say. Remember that your Brother told you to companion those "willing to leave hell behind." He may have only asked this of you personally in this way, Mari, but he asked over a dozen times in A Course of Love *that heaven be chosen over hell, and described what this might look like. But even that is different than "leaving hell behind."*

Embracing the unity of the feminine and masculine will begin the dissolution of other divisions carried within, and in doing so, make it possible for hell to be left behind. In the Embrace, you will respond naturally and be received personally and with kinship. **We, together, return intimacy to an impersonal world.** *We act out of a realm that is just a misty step away from the partially insane and bounded world we serve to save. We respond with the love that is who we are, in the ways that we are given to bestow love, and in the love that gives us our voices, our sovereignty, and allows us to offer each other revelation. We rejoin with holy harmony as we sing the new song that creates the New Earth in the Universe and births The New out of each divine mother's womb.*

From the two together comes the One.

My favorite version of this idea, or warning of it, Mother, is from the first chapter of *A Course of Love*: "Striving to be that which you can never be is the hell you have created."*

My Mari, I have used the word "compose" perfectly. Treat our dialogue, and each dialogue in the same way. What comes of two together is the way whose time has come.

In Love ever increasing, never perfected . . . always free and out of bounds of the old . . . we open the Way that will free you from the hackles of ordinary time. We free you for Metanoia's revolution in consciousness.

We leave the time that has been, and speak, in this Advent of The New, of the way of the Word in the tongue of our Mother Love.

Your Holy Mary, Mother of the Living.

And now all has become quiet. Very quiet.

---

* *ACOL* C:1.13

A WAY OF REFLECTION

My dear ones, when you believe in hard reality, you put faith in the non-existent. My way is a way of reflection, and a reflection is what an image is. The deep significance of your faith in imagination is faith in the image—faith in the image freed from logic and the ego's literalism.

Right now, there is a parting going on. Falling apart is an imaginal process.

We, of the feminine nature, are associated with alchemy for the un-forming, not the forming. In letting the old fall apart, and in shedding the formulaic, you enter the realm in which meaning isn't "made for you" or even made by you. Here, you find knowing that "comes to you" and is full of significance as what it is. It is not the meaning "of" anything. It is less meaningful than imaginal, less indicator than message. In this way, all thought of "meaning" begins to fall away. It's time to let this happen.

In ACOL *your Brother described what comes to you as "a glimpse of fleeting light in darkness" that "provides for a knowing of light."*[*] *In* ACIM *he spoke of faith as "the messenger of the new perception, sent forth to gather witnesses unto its coming and to return their messages to you."*[†]

This reminds me that I had a long letter from Michael Mark which caused my own longest letter in a while, starting with a question

---

[*] *ACOL* D:Day18.5

[†] *ACIM* T-19.I.11

about the idea of creative tension and the sense that disagreement and discord can produce more fruitful ideas and outcomes.

I love the way he and I spark each other.

I'm not sure why, but our exchange brought to mind Martin Luther King, Jr.'s *Letter from a Birmingham Jail*, and how he said Jesus and other great reformers were extremists. He wrote that "the question is not whether we will be extremists, but what kind of extremists we will be. Will we be extremists for hate or for love?"[*]

---

[*] "Letter from a Birmingham Jail [King Jr.]" *African Stuies Center – University of Pennsylvania*.
https://www.africa.upenn.edu/Articles_Gen/Letter_Birmingham.html.
Accessed March 9, 2024.

𝒯HE NEW IS THE CHALLENGE OF EVERY AGE

Getting back to myself, I think of how the philosopher Martin Heidegger called for a "'special hermeneutic of empathy' to dissolve the classic philosophic issue of 'other minds' by putting the issue in the context of the being-with of human relatedness."* I have a sense that this didn't go well for him. The *Wikipedia* article I found on this topic noted there were those who claimed that "such texts are conventionalized expressions of the experience of the author." Apparently, it was shocking that the experience of an author might inform the science of the author! It still is in many instances. And not just in the scientific field.

How many of the most inspired and forward-looking figures in history were fought for challenging what was already known? And fought, particularly, when their discoveries were made through their own experience. The experience of the person has been systematically removed from science and is suspect in academia generally. The same is often true in spirituality and religion.

Does this still make sense? When our most beloved psychologists, such as Jung, so clearly discovered so much out of their own psyches? Does it make sense for any human experience to be summarily discounted?

I'm so thankful that I could cry when I learn of those who persevered, and those who support original knowing, especially the

---

* "Hermeneutics." *Wikipedia*. https://en.wikipedia.org/wiki/Hermeneutics. Accessed March 9, 2024.

kind that can't be categorized. It's like what I, and we, must do to keep the way open for The New, in whatever way it comes to us. This, "Mary's way" is only one way. But it extends from the page, and if it resonates with you, it will spin into your life, changing *your* life in time, and your contribution to changing *time* in life.

The Second Coming:
Life as It's Self

ℳETANOIA: REVOLUTION, REVELATION & REALITY

My Mary, I don't know what I'm doing with Metanoia. But you spoke this to me in *Mirari*:

In your daily life you are beset by forgetting, beset to such a degree that it begins to concern you. You see remembering and forgetting as opposites. But this is the way of old. Forgetting also reveals love's life in you.*

You say that remembering and forgetting are not opposites, and I know, even as my forgetting makes my life difficult, that what you say is true. Although I can't explain it, the following, also from *Mirari*, feels like the clearest descriptor of Metanoia that I can think of:

Your heart holds a reflection of your soul. The cells in your body, and their interaction, mirror the activity in the heavens. You are not separate from anything.†

Is this what's happening? Is Metanoia the creation of a new reality in which the union of the within and without is naturally recognized? Oh, Mary, I really feel that, see that.

Yes, this is what is being revealed now. As in the past, revelation is more the experience of the few than the many. As the miracle can't be

---

* *Mirari*, p. 247

† *Ibid.*, p. 157

ordered, revelation also can't be ordered. But the miracle is an act of mutual revelation. Revelation spreads the miraculous.

I love that, Mary.

Metanoia is the miracle of the "great turning" in time and space. Your friend's choice of that song came of the connection of which we speak, and became an act of mutual revelation. Union within and without—union with one another—is already a part of how many women (and some men) naturally think and act. This union furthers the revolution, a revolution that is also a measure of time. Time and miracles share a true creative union, that comes of abiding, as you say, "in and within." It is being "in and within" that produces a sudden, radical, and complete change that is as choiceless as it is mutual. It speaks to what is already drawing you.

Listen. What is beckoning? What call are you hearing in your psychic depths? Here, you might remember that Jesus asks you to rely on your desire for what you already are, your given and beloved Self. You also can recall that when we speak of time we also speak of the action of celestial bodies going about in their orbits. "Here," we expand the realm of the Self.

This reminds me of what creation is, Mary, and what it may be more fully, in The New "time of Christ." Jesus spoke of it as "our power":

What this portion of the dialogue attempts to do is to give you a language to support what you already know, and are already aware of, so that you are more comfortable with letting what you know serve you in your creation of [T]he [N]ew. All—all—that you need in order to create [T]he [N]ew is available within you. The power of the universe is given and received constantly in support of the creation of [T]he [N]ew. This is what creation is! The entire universe, the All of All, giving and receiving as one. This is our power. And our power is needed for the creation of the Covenant of The New in this time of Christ.[*]

Metanoia's revolution is of an orbital realm in which what you imagine, envision, and desire will come to be . . . You. Imagine your Self in this orbit where your heart holds a reflection of your soul. Imagine yourself on its path—the orbital path of one body as it revolves around another.

Being is personified not only by soul, but by angels, by spirit, by the stars . . . and by your Earth, your planet that is currently in such distress. This is why you find yourself personifying that which is of your plot of ground. Your planet Earth needs to join the imaginal in the sacred realm of boundlessly personified being to reveal the soul of the world.

The Holy Relationship you have with the All of Everything is here to embrace you and help you come to be . . . You. As this happens in you, it happens "in" your world and "to" your world.

"Dwelling," in the imaginal sense, is being in an imaginal "state of being." As you say, Mari, "it's an atmosphere"—like that of the stars that take you beyond influence and let you encounter your worth. "Here," the many who deeply, deeply want to walk out from behind the walls they have erected can be seen without the push and pull that destabilizes. Now there is a new view, inner and outer and beyond. The one appears to the one, each in their imaginal glory: unity regained.

"Here" expands in this turn to The New. As tender voices stoke the fire with their fresh and heartfelt language, they remind each other

---

[*] see *ACOL* D3.23

to feed no more egos, and to return no more to that orbit. I will not leave you at the mercy of that which would destroy. No. You and I are here for the tender, for the fragile new life birthing into being—those, male and female, who are ready to be revealed in truth. These are those prepared to be made known in the orbital path of love.

Now, the tender-hearted can realize the strength in their fragility. They have patterned themselves anew. There is nothing, nothing stronger than the tender heart, the heart of the mother in the celestial presence of mother/father love for protection of the new babe.

In recognition then, one-to-another, courage will be found, a signal will be given. You will look the great deceiver in the eye and stand firmly in your own orbit where all gentled souls will recognize the heart's knowing . . . for the sake of The New.

For the sake of The New, the new orbit is not all about being known. When needed, it will provide anonymity. It will be like invisibility. It can present as androgyne. You are incorruptible—uninfluenced by the old. Your identity is certain even as it is changing. Time outside of time has arrived in you.

And now your beneficence rises.

Recouping the Loss of Holy Relationship Through Creation of the New

Accepting the true frustrates the false. Denying the old makes room for creation of The New. We are doing this right now. This is our united purpose.

You are not alone. You can do this.

Here, in the time of recognition that creation of The New must proceed, you are to take up your mantle to dismiss and shield yourselves from the order that has been. Metanoia will proceed without creating a new order. Its revolutionary offering is freedom and protection of the new babe.

You will recognize *those who are ready.*

Now, as people seek—most unknowingly—for the undefinable something that they know is missing, they will begin to find that relational thriving is the only thriving.

There is a similar movement about to happen in books.

The interest you still have in books from the 1990's and before, is due to those that didn't confine themselves to soulless descriptions of the psyche. Most did not try to prescribe methods or teach what could not be taught. They would not attempt to make you healthy in a way compatible with a blueprint of health—mental, physical, or spiritual—but would help accelerate your recognition that a return to your true nature would, of itself, restore you.

You were most taken, in A Course in Miracles, *by its talk of Holy Relationship. But if you weren't in the minority then, you certainly are now. You were enveloped, at the time, by holy relationship with your "spirit sisters" Mary Love and Julieanne Carver, so when you read of it, it was with enthusiasm and a feeling of validation for what you'd found. You already knew that you wanted to live and create and . . . be . . . in Holy Relationship. The beginning of this revolution in consciousness will take those like yourself, and the extension of Holy Relationship, to recoup this interpersonal loss.*

Metanoia's great turning cannot happen in those intent on directing the manner of return. Do you see? Following direction is what got humanity into the very crisis in which it is in. In the years we've been writing together, direction from the loudest of voices is what has received the most attention. Those teeming with painful anger are revealing only their failure to thrive. Being wealthy and powerful is rarely a measure of thriving. The bullies who once reigned in school playgrounds grow into bullies who hold sway on a scale that is enormously destructive. This difficult reality must be seen if you are to understand the great necessity of a revolution that extends beyond the physical and is anchored by the expansive and soulful qualities of the feminine in men as well as women.

Knowing With

It's 5:38, and here in the cabin it is utterly black both inside and outside the window. The dark is my primordial beginning, my alleluia call to pre-dawn inspiration, my desire for union in the way of the duad. The way of the duad is, in some manner, the ground of the beginning—those spaces between two that let sprouts rise from the earth, and the babe peek out of the womb. They're the "pre" of pre-existence, the pre that was before the dawn of a *known* world. The pre of our Holy Ones, from whom life arose and still arises. The pre of the unnamable.

What is generally spoken of as our known world isn't known at all, only named. I don't know the proper names of some of my trees but I *know* my trees. I once wanted to know all their given names—asked for a tree book one Christmas, looked for an app for my phone. It wasn't accidental that neither came to be. It's not their names I need to know, but them. I need to know they live along with me and are of the same fabric. My quest is not the naming, or the knowing that is "knowledge of," but "knowing with."

This *is* the revelation that is our Heritage.

The Third-Something and Holy Relationship

Jesus also called this way the "third something."

[T]his all-encompassing relationship, both within you and without you, both you and all you are in relationship with, is that third something that is the holy relationship.*

The "third something" is what happens in our Holy Relationships with each other, with God, nature, in dialogue, in creativity, and in what can materialize "here" when "together" we come to new and holy knowing that is mine, that is yours, *and* that is "ours" . . . of Heaven and of Earth.

We are the beloved creators, the authors of a new time. A way that disregards the newness being offered neglects the whole of what is offered: the way *to* The New and the announcement *of* The New. Many of us, along with Mother Mary, are feminine architects of The New, calling men as well as women to step up into this new time and to disrupt the hierarchy.

Each one, being noticeably true to who they are and all they love, will counteract the disregard, even without proclamations.

Jesus came from God, but never said, "God says."

He said, "I am in my Father and my Father in me."

Suddenly "I" can see that this is the way it is. Now it is about us and our Brother and Mother and the Holy Ones of every religious

---

* *ACOL* T2:12.9

and spiritual family of love. We rest in each other and birth with each other.

What we do . . . here . . . now, is create the atmosphere in which this radical love in us can be realized and its message made clear. I ask all called to be creators of The New, to keep their council close in order not to invite the architecture of the old. The old architecture is always once removed: *he said, she said.* This is our call to create the new *text*, the new *architecture,* and to do it with the alchemy that is part of manifesting in a new way.

Speaking of this in *Memoria*, Mary said, *"This is not the manifesting itself. This is not construction. This is setting down in memory the vision of which we speak. In it is implied all that, like the spacing of the cosmos, will hold the vision of The New."**

For vision is like love, and this is not only compassionate or creative love. This love is ardently, rigorously, courageously, the radical love of the feminine. As her or his body embraces the Christed-Self within, "she/he," along with Mother Earth, become the carriers of the new babe.

ℳ

My life feels like a parable. When I couldn't quite claim my knowing as my own, this showed me something, just as it has shown many women: "It was not allowed." I was losing myself in "the voice," but first by my own hand. I had to be coaxed (by Jesus and then Mary) into not removing myself. How many times have we been coached

---

* *Memoria*, p. 250

to an opposite end? But good God! If we have to leave humility behind to be honest, to no longer accept our removal, so be it.

It is no wonder we of the feminine have been angry. We are original in our knowing. As "this work" originated in me, your work originates in you. As my realization of "being in union" is mine, yours is yours. This recognition has been long awaited by our Holy Ones. Your realization of your "being" in "union" with "your" Holy Ones and holy work, is what you may now have found, or still await. And sometimes you only "await it" because you feel it's not allowed. There are occasions when we feel we can't claim what isn't sanctioned. Other times, we don't allow ourselves to feel what we feel. Neither can continue if we are to be creators of The New.

You will no longer need to "think" about who you are and what you will do, and your willingness to give up this thinking will be paramount to your realization that everything has changed or that nothing has changed.*

---

* *ACOL* D:E.14

𝒯HE SOUL RETURNS HOME

I follow the coming of morning the way I do. It's my morning reverie. I love these days when reverie is really what I'm in. I'll have to look up the word later. Could it replace thinking and thought and all the mental words? Could reverie mean "to revere"?

How long has it been since I've said in a "reverential" way how much I love the coming of day? How I align myself with the coming of day, the coming.

Oh, my Lord, the second coming. The Second Coming!!

We live there now! In the second coming!

Oh, Holy Ones, have I sat here so long that I finally see?

The Way of Mary is a prelude to the personification of the holy.

The time of the Second Coming is here.

Life is the first Coming. Life as Its Self is the second coming. This second coming is what God the Mother and Mother Earth facilitate. Here, on this Earth, you are held in the womb of the Great Mother.*

---

* *Memoria*, p. 72 (emphasis added)

The End of Defense & Lamentations

This "new life" I'm experiencing is going to take some getting used to. A life in which I'm not defending myself.

I have to say it again: not defending myself.

I'll have to thank Kate for helping me see how defended I have been. Kate and you. And me. And Jesus. Everything and everyone who brought me to this place where I can quit. If I can. I have never realized how used to being defended I am . . . even while it is less than it once was. Now, I can mourn the times of innocence when my hackles weren't raised too. Those times before I knew I needed defense, and this time in which I am experiencing it in reverse, the trap that it is.

I laugh. I was "set up" to see this by being given a "new course in miracles." How could I defend that!

I've had this idea, my Mother, of "laments." There is Jeremiah, in the Bible, giving voice to grief at the destruction of Jerusalem. There is still such grieving going on in that area of the world. Likely in every part of the world. Maybe it would be good for all to lament.

Lamentations.

They—lamentations—are so much of what I write when I journal.

But not all. Lamentations are a counterpoint to the wonder of life. The wonder, the Mirari of life, both invites and stills the lamentations because it has re-opened the wounded heart and given it a voice. Lamentations reveal that you can sustain grace in the midst of suffering. It is only when lamenting is not allowed that people fall into a despair from which they can see no exit.

Can you feel the power of your morning time, now? Your morning time has included all the movements of the human heart, the movements that bring about this revolution in consciousness.

The Beyond Within

I realize every day, Mary, how "the personal" is such a challenging way to be. Laws are static. Belief can be too. But the personal is fluid, every day, every hour, distinct to each relationship, moving backward and forward in time. How we feel it all is beyond me.

Then I realize: It "is" beyond us. This "beyond" is the gift of soul and its imagination. It's what makes us spacious.

With our revolution of consciousness, the universe of the soul creates free space within which "we" become "its" embodiment. The impersonality given to "the great beyond" is false because it is the "beyond within" where our soul abides.

ℰPIPHANY

January 6, 2021

Last year, on this day, the Epiphany event that occurred at the U.S. Capitol* was underway. In remembrance of the riot this year, the Senate chaplain, Barry C. Black, spoke of the power of words:

These tragedies have reminded us that words matter, and that the power of life and death is in the tongue. We have been warned that eternal vigilance continues to be freedom's price.†

He also noted that the Lord has helped us "remember that we need to see in each other a common humanity that reflects [His] image," and petitioned Him to bring "healing and unity to our hurting and divided nation and world" through one another.

You have foreseen,‡ since the beginning of this journey at the start of Advent 1998, this New Advent. You foresaw the end of ordinal time. You did not know what you foresaw or see it as a foreseeing because it came by way of words. But you are of the tradition of the Word. This is not a failing. It is not less because it is not the vision of your eyes. "The Word" speaks of vision beyond the eyes. Do you not yet realize this?

---

* Following the defeat of then U.S. President Donald Trump in the 2020 presidential election.

† Clark, Barry C. "Closing Prayer." Joint Session of United States Congress, January 7, 2021, Washington, D.C. Prayer Reading.

‡ see *Mirari*, p. 189

At that time, I said that this—being of the way of the Word—"was still a *dawning* realization," but I've accepted it now. It never made me feel shy or awkward as some of the other nice things you've said about me did. Then . . . you also spoke of the inception of New Life as the starting point of what is here and still to come: the living Christ.[*]

And that is the antidote to time continuing on in the way it has been. I know you are saying to yourself, "It always comes back to that . . . being true to Self." And as big as that is, we revealed even more.

Be no longer causeless?

Yes!

You are in grace and union with the Source and Cause of unity. Be no longer causeless. You and your Source are one.[†]

You would not be happy if you were causeless, and you know this. You are dedicated to "our" cause now, which is not the whole of which this passage spoke, but as with the past, the whole contains all parts, and we are rapidly putting parts together in the frame of The New— for cause. Your cause has narrowed and expanded at once with our Way of Mary.

Yes, I see that . . . the women, the new babe, the revolution in consciousness, Metanoia and the imaginal. The feminine, held by a new strength of will in men as well as women. The way of the word to convey it all.

Many shoots of light, my Mari.

---

[*] *Ibid.*, p. 189

[†] *ACOL* D:Day1.13

DO NOT LOOK FOR CAUSE

You bring your sad heart here, even when you tell yourself you have no cause for sadness. What would happen if you did not look for cause?

Oh, the notion of everything having a cause. It's an errant idea, isn't it?

Only in the way you look at it . . . as if you are in charge of cause and effect. As your Brother said, "It's the joining that is real. . . . No one thing exists without another. Cause and effect are one."*

Mother, that's also when Jesus said "We are beginning now to paint you a new picture, a picture of things unseen before but visible to your heart if not your eyes. Your heart knows love without a vision of it."† How I appreciated that! What is visible to our hearts!

Yes, we continue to bring forward the ways in which you "think you know" and the ways you truly know. And I want to share with you that, strangely enough, "cause and effect" and "use and abuse" speak for us about the same matter, but as opposites. And I ask you to realize—to really take in—that words "speak for us." They are the major form of communication—universally—between humans. It is how humans convey who they are and how they feel . . . via the Word. And I speak of myself as human here, too. This is what we propose for all: to be human and divine.

This is important to talk about for how essential it is, my sons and daughters, to embrace your words with feeling. I speak of this

---

* *ACOL* C:5.6

† *ACOL* C:5.7

because, although Jesus described the positive side of cause and effect, when you ask, "What is this for?" you are looking for cause to have a particular, predetermined effect. I want you to be ready for this to cease altogether with the end of learning. You will know, and at times "know what you know," but you will at times, know without knowing what you know. That's the unknown knowing.

Oh Mother, this has been such a rich morning! Our direction so unexpected! I love it when that happens. I recognize all you say about unknown knowing.

Taking on the Same Nature

My mood as we begin today is wistful, and I wish for a sky as reflective as my feelings.

You prefer a sky in harmony with your mood.

I do! The dark is more embracing—to me—of me. It's me and the dark. Two as one. Not a cacophony of this and that. In a brighter mood, the green and all the movement of the trees is a feast. But not today. It's not that I feel sad, only that I'm glad of being in a ... soulful mood. I wanted to come up with something more positive to call it than sadness.

But does it need to be positive? That's the thing. That's my underlying question.

Do you know the strength it takes not to cheer up? Not to be artificially gladdened? To know that you need the sad song rather than the one that cheers you? "Does it need to be positive?" may be the best question you've asked.

As if it can only be one or the other.

Yes! And emotions are seen, in this polarity, as positive or negative. They are pleasant or unpleasant. Sad or happy. Either/or rather than both/and. This is another area in which Metanoia invites change. Either/or propositions are always limiting. You wrote of this with Jesus in A Course of Love *and how those who feel separate define every relationship in this way.*[*]

I feel this, Mother, feel the truth of the limitation it is to think in either/or fashion. I am one with this cabin and these woods, and

---

[*] see *ACOL* D:Day37.3

with each creation I bring forth. This is not only my reality but "the" reality, and to me, the truth of what creation is. It's the way of the Creator and the way all of creation comes into being. Jesus said that "giving ideas life is the role of creatorship," and that "our first creation is, in a sense, creation, or recreation of [our]selves."*

It's the creation part I like the most, and in the next day of our dialogue Jesus speaks of "accepting the end of choice and the beginning of creation."† It's one of my favorite phrases from *A Course of Love*. And it's there in a like manner in *ACIM* too: "Choosing *means* divided will."‡ This tells me that my response is my creation. The way I live is my creation. What I make of my life is of my creatorship. Our creations are birthed just like our children are. This is our mirroring of the human and divine together as one. Now, as men and women receive this revolutionary "right" to be who we are, we "let it in," and we respond with care and devotion to The New that is created.

But it's not all that easy.

---

* *ACOL* D:Day35.10-11
† *ACOL* D:Day36.18
‡ *ACIM OE* T:5.23

The Incoming

It's not easy because of the framework that has been built around your emotions. The learning framework sees emotions, thoughts and feelings dichotomously and this is a result of the thinking mind's polarization. Everything is either/or, and this is not the case. It is not always the case that anger is bad. It's not always the case that seeking personal peace is good. Sadness is not bad and happiness good. All of this either/or thinking is the result of what's been taught, from earliest childhood on. It's why it was so revolutionary when Jesus spoke of anger in The Dialogues. *You were rather thunderstruck, and yet the way he threw out the pursuit of saintly notions—of always remaining in peace, or always accepting "others" over yourself—drew up such love and thankfulness in you! You'd suffered so much from being "nice" that you knew this already . . . but hadn't known you knew it. Do you see? There are many meanings to knowing what you don't think you know. Metanoia pushes these boundaries.*

It's akin to the in-between time that's been my love. And that might be significant to the way I see things, to who I am, and to this writing we do, Mary. Before you, I didn't recognize the in-between as I do now. I think I "felt it" but didn't "know it." I had my "cave" room during my time with Jesus, so this communing with nature is new to our dialogue. I didn't know, until my time with you, that my longing for the cabin had anything to do with the in-between. I just knew I wanted time alone and a place to write undisturbed. And that, in itself, is an expression that could be taken in multiple ways: as time "by" myself, time "to" myself, or only as time. Longing for time of my own.

Oh my God, I suddenly remember one of the first expressions of the angel Peace when he came to me in 1995: "Don't try to force it, to will it, just let it come. It is there **in the in-between,** between thought and feeling. Breathe. Feel your heart."*

It's there in the in-between! I knew it then! Why am I only claiming it now? Who would I be if I had any memory at all, my Holy Ones? Why do I only seem to stumble backwards to see in a true manner?

If you must have a reason, ask yourself if you would be who you are meant to be if you were delivering the way of the Word . . . in A Course of Love, in Mirari, in Memoria, in this narrative on Metanoia . . . in a manner not meant to be. **Nothing is premeditated. What you write here is happening to you, it is occurring. It is an event.** *You aren't intended to compose a narrative on your own, to be a scholar of your own work, or to go it alone. You are here for the incoming. The incoming arises from Holiness. You're meant to hold The New like the pregnant woman holds her child. To be in love with it and carry it "within you" to its time of readiness for the birth. And then to gather in elation of the birth. Readers would do themselves a service if they saw reading in this fashion.*

You were, Mari, innocent enough to not be invested in what you received in a way inappropriate to it.

Remember your experience writing Creation of the New. *You took on the vague and wind-like character of the in-between, of what makes its presence known, but is not seen. Don't you see?* **In these states, you take on the same nature. Taking on the same nature is part of being natural in a way that is of The New,** *and at the*

---

* *Peace, Book III of The Grace Trilogy,* p. 35

same time is a way that is as old as time and memory. It is the feeling of "not in one place," the "not all here," as you sometimes say.

I can imagine that, Mary, because I feel that what you're saying is true—at least I do after contemplating it for a minute. But also, what we do is like a combining of your time and mine. A melding.

Yes, my daughter. And when life is lived in this way, "time" is flexible.

THE ALL OF EVERYTHING & THE VOID OF NOTHING

Suddenly, Jesus is with me.

"Remember," he says, "that as we began, I was pointing to the fallacies of the *interpretations* that came after *A Course in Miracles*. 'The Course' of *A Course of Love* was, and is, a needed rebuttal, a correction of the incorrect before the 'all of everything' or the 'void of nothing' could be opened to you. Recall that, as we entered the 40 Days, I told you that 'You can be both/and, rather than either/or.'"[*]

Thank you, Jesus. It seems somewhat like the "natural" promise I associate with my love for "the in-between." Isn't something in-between not quite one or the other? Could this also have a similar meaning to "time outside of time," with its murkiness, and indefinability? I hadn't thought of it that way, but now I wonder. I speak of it mainly because of my own feeling of being between worlds.

How beautifully put, my sister. That idea, that vision, is of You. It is Your vision.

But your question now calls me to talk of spaciousness with you. What our Mother suggested was finding what she called "a common location" . . . a location "within spaciousness." She was speaking of the connection that comes from our union—of us being together "in the same place." It is the same with the joining of the realms. I told you once that if your scientists knew what to look for,

---

[*] *ACOL* D:Day10.21

they would find it,* and in your dialogue with our Mother she said, "We are breaching the space that scientists have yet to discover."† Metanoia's revolution brings you closer to your discovery of our in-common location in Oneness.

Every imaginal idea comes to you from this place outside of time. It is also true that each imaginal idea can only meet you where you are. Metanoia thus brings the starting place and the meeting place . . . together.

You have always wondered about this, and now I'll confirm your wondering: The end of ordinal time *is* the end of *chronological* time . . . and more. Chronology is arranged by order of occurrence. So, what could be more revolutionary to your consciousness than for it to be taken outside of time's chronology? To remove it from the confines it has been held within? The confines that humanity has forgotten are unnatural?

Remember that the end of ordinal time "in you" is the revolution that was sparked by your return to Love through *A Course of Love*. Now, with Mother love, you have found wonder (Mirari) and memories (Memoria) including those of time outside of time. Here you are beginning to realize your readiness and even eagerness to experience Metanoia's revolution "in time."

This combination causes you to become conscious, in a way natural *to you*, that you have entered the spaciousness of time outside of time. Metanoia rises in you as your consciousness continues to accept, and live, in this spaciousness, *within* time. You are already feeling it. You just didn't recall the language in which it was foretold. This is partially due to wholeness. You were called

---

* *ACOL* D:Day6.21
† *Memoria*, p. 315

to "wholeness," not to the "recall of wholeness." You were asked "to end the time of learning" but not of "discovery." Discovery "is the new divine pattern." It replaces the "thought systems" we spoke of in our *Course*. "To discover is simply to find out what you did not previously know."* And that's what's needed for The New to come into being.

Revelation cannot come to those who are so "certain" of what *is* that they cannot allow for the new to be revealed. Your certainty about what *is* is a false certainty, a learned certainty based on the fear that caused you to order the world according to a set of facts and rules. Be jubilant rather than hesitant about the time of discovery that is before you.†

I so love being in the time of discovery, but what you call spaciousness feels more like spacy-ness to me.

You make me laugh, my sister. As you have been realizing, this is an enormous shift in the way you know, the very alteration that hangs in the air like the mist you are seeing at this moment. It is so fine you wonder if it is real or unreal. Physical or imaginal. Actual or mirage. Yet, you know what you see, and have "seen." This is similar to what we have been working on. The transformation that changes your experience from "one" level of time to one of experiencing "two" levels of time. Soon you will no longer ask if it is one or the other. You are already beginning to see in a both/and manner. There is no need to worry, only to know that this—this that you experience newly—is the way of The New.

---

* *ACOL* D:6.14
† *ACOL* D:6.15-16

Thank you so much, my dear Jesus. Your words have made this clear to me.

𝒯HE PROMISE OF THE SPACIOUS SELF

When we spoke of the "possibility" of light becoming the "presence" of light, we spoke of it as gently unraveling the threads of time.* The promise of the Spacious Self is one of recognizing and living within the light that spaciousness has opened to you.

Thank you so much, my Brother and Mother. You have advanced my understanding of what I experience, and you've shared love with me today. They are the same. I don't say that often enough—how I feel "the love" in your words, and how they are then delivered to a place deep within me. They sustain me and my love for you, and even, sometimes, my love for me.

You spoke to me earlier of accepting the relationship of Christ into my own being, and called it a cooperative relationship of all with everything. You said it abides within and that I, and we, can't decide what "to do with it," but can only be it.†

Oh, my Lord! Has what I've felt as "the in-between" been that of the Time of Christ?

Sister, now is the proper moment for you to realize that "you" have created, from the in-between, a space that is filled with the energy of Christ—the same energy that accompanied my entrance into this dimension of human and divine unity. You took the step of accepting *the relationship of the between***, which is the feminine way.**

I'm really stunned, Jesus, and feel so small and inadequate. Have I gotten it wrong all this time?

---

* excerpts from ACOL D:Day28.20 and 22

† see *ACOL* D:E.16

My sister . . . no! You've gotten it, let's say, in context—in context, Mari. Context *is* a weaving together of words. Remember that I added "A Note on Being" to our *Course of Love* specifically to clarify this.

What you "realize" now you truly "make real" as your being applies love's extension to all with whom you are in relationship.

You will no longer need to "think" about who you are and what you will do, and your willingness to give up this thinking will be paramount to your realization that everything has changed or that nothing has changed.

These are both possibilities, as all possibilities are yours. Which do you choose?

There is no longer an in-between unless you create it. You have taken the step of accepting the relationship of the between, the relationship of Christ, into your own being. The cooperative relationship of all with everything abides within you now. You do not, and cannot decide what to do with it, you can only be it. This is the choice you have made. To be. So be it.*

I might already be a pro at not thinking, Jesus!

What I feel I've heard is that we are still weaving with words . . . but now we are weaving in the pattern of The New . . . which, just maybe, doesn't include thought, or at least not "thought as we've known it"!

---

* *ACOL* D:E.13-16

"You see," Mary says, *"you haven't forgotten! You have carried all you have received within you—to ready our work for its birth into the world."*

You and Jesus have both reminded us that all you've spoken of is also in an in-between time because it's "in us" now. It is animated along with us, comes into being along with the "new Self" we each encounter, and becomes the place this new Self can be realized. We "exist in acceptance and union, rather than in learning and separation." Our encounters exist in love, and don't come about from changes in our external circumstances but from changes in our internal perspective.*

It coincides, Mary, with what you said to me about being a chronicler of time.

In a sense, Mari, we're speaking of you being a chronicler of time's demise . . . in you. You are in a dimension of "that was then, this is now" and this is what you are chronicling. You didn't quite get this before, but you're getting it now, which is perfect, and the only way anyone truly "gets" anything: It dawns on you. Remember what I shared with you earlier of time's relationship to events within each person's "experience" of time. I was not speaking of "clock" time.

You say this just as the sun's time-keeping chases me to the edge of the table once again. I have a feeling this has to do with each of our own natural cycles, just like that of the sun, moon, and stars. I see that the clock-time that was "then" is not now.

Yes! And what do you suppose will happen in the world as natural cycles return to divinely human Beings? It's going to disrupt a few things, my daughter. How could it not?

---

* see *ACOL* D:Day7.8

I love how you take so many of my "ordinary life" dilemmas and transport them into another dimension where they have meaning beyond the ordinary.

It is love moving you in this direction, Mari. Changing time is disruptive. It throws "phases or levels," as Yeshua says, "into disorder." To disrupt time is to cause it to break down, to crack the stones of culture. The disturbances establish a breach in what was and shatter the peace you could only achieve through taking your place in the previous order. Changing time is also what allows space for The New to come. This is the bigger picture represented in many smaller pictures within the same frame. Remember it. **This change in time is what allows The New to come.**

Waking Dreams & Metanoia's Internal Revolution

One day, when Donny wanted to record the square footage of Henry's old upstairs room as being heated for "Course" purposes, he asked, "What do I call that?"

I said, "I call it the 'Jesus Room.'"

He said, "How about the 'Receiving Room'?"

I thought both statements, mine and his, were pretty remarkable. I would not have said "the Jesus Room" six months ago, and I would not have known he knew the word "receiving."

In that room, receiving *A Course of Love* from Jesus is what occurred. I needed to be shut-in, sequestered. I never looked out the window. With you, Mary, it's been a great deal of window time . . . whether here in the cabin, or at the dining room table, or in the sunroom. When *ACOL* was being written, the sunroom was the TV room!

"Then," I needed to get my "thinking mind" out of the way so I could focus only on what Jesus wanted to share with me. "Now" I have needed to open my whole being . . . really my whole life . . . for the cause of openness I suppose. For union and relationship. Hell, who am I kidding? For healing.

It's 7:05 in the cabin and I've seen the first bunny out here—a really big fellow, bigger than a good-sized cat. The sky is bluer now than when I arrived, and remains utterly still. We're not in the "safe zone" yet that generally comes around mid-March: We could still get another snowstorm. But the signs of spring are here, all but the green. How lovely it will be to have the green come.

Every once in a while, I feel like an undiscovered prophet with our writing, Mary. But when I reread what we've done, as I've been doing the last few days, I don't see it. I wonder why people are so impacted. Only the diversity of those who have found our words inspiring reassures me that there is power here for others besides me. Well, not *only* that. I have dared, along with you, to be original. I know you are origin incarnate, and I believe in the unrepeatability of the person. It's you and Jesus who call each of us who "are The New," in and of ourselves, not to "do" something New, but to "be" The New. I'm so grateful to be doing this with you!

Thank you for letting me see that this morning, Holy Mother.

I wonder if I don't dream at night because I am in the realm of dreams during the day. Being with you is somewhat like a waking dream.

That's a good way to put it. You, and many of my sons and daughters open to unity, are entering the realm of dreams in your waking state. I know you wish for more sleeping dreams as they've been such heralds to your work with the divine, but do not dismiss the waking dream state. It is not "only" between us, but it is between us.

I suspect I couldn't dismiss it even if I wanted to. But it's not as clear cut, Mary. Waking dreams are not, or feel as though they're not, totally beyond my volition.

Do you suppose sleeping dreams are not the same?

What do you imagine volition to be? I can see why you would question it, as volition is an act of will, which we have yet to speak of. We have not spoken of "to wish" or "to will." When you think of a "wish" you see something sweet and simple and beyond your effort. But when you think of "will" you associate it with the power of choice and with determination. Since we are done with that, it is time to see waking dreams newly, and to see "will" separately from your concept of will power or "will to power."

That sounds fascinating and is a surprising turn. So often I feel like your guidance follows my conscious need. This feels like revelation of a need I didn't know I had. I do like the word "wish." I'm not as sure of "will."

Let's stay with "wish" then, for a while.

We continue, following love's course in you, and the forward movement of the currents of its imaginal realms. The beauty of "wishes" is their power, by way of their subconscious nature, to rise gently into consciousness. You sit in this cabin today because of a wish that rose to consciousness "out of nowhere" in 2003. You didn't know you wanted a cabin until suddenly it was a great yearning that rose in this way. Your exploration of the imaginal is much the same. After your "experience" of the imaginal "rising" within A Course of Love,[*] *you encountered a draw that you did not understand but that you let lead your experience.*

That is so true! It was as though I fell in love with the very word *imaginal*. How could I not? And part of its appeal was that I didn't know what it was or what it meant. And there was no information to be found about it at that time. It had the feeling of something undiscovered. And because of my experience within "The Embrace," I took it personally. That makes a big difference. When something in *A Course of Love* would affect me that "strongly" it always arose from a "meant for me" feeling. Which, of course, doesn't mean exclusive. I would guess that "The Embrace" was one of the favorite chapters for many readers and that the appeal of the

---

[*] Mary refers to my personal experience receiving the chapter in *ACOL* entitled "The Embrace."

imaginal may have come to life in them too. The original excitement I felt over it is still "in me" in that way it originally arrived, like a great yearning. I might not see this differently than wishes and dreams, but I would see it contrary to will.

Why do you say that, Mari?

Because, to me, "will" has a sense of force . . . or at least intent.

Which is why you may not have been able to see it in its supportive aspects, and why you have felt so unsupported all these years. Imagine a human being without the will to live. Without the will to thrive. Without the will to create.

Aren't all these aspects of will necessary? And aren't each of them in areas in which you have felt unsupported? Can you accept, now, your will to live, your will to thrive, your will to dream and to create, as well as to explore this revolution of The New? Will supports your spiritual transformation. You, and many, need to accept that your life-force, your very will to live as who you are, is keenly alive and yearning to receive your attention. Metanoia's internal revolution ushers in The New, but it can only "await" you until you are ready. Are you ready?

ℒOVE'S SWEETNESS: IN RECOVERY

Mary, I think that's the first time I've felt your full power enter our words.

Do you remember, Mari, that the angel Peace greeted you with "sweetness,"* and that when Jesus provided you with an introduction to A Course of Love, *he spoke of love and its sweetness?† That introduction, which your Brother gave you only years after the work of* ACOL *had been completed, could be seen as both a recap of your experience and a new philosophy in concert with feminine will.*

In it, you also heard,

"Everyone" is just a concept. These words are given to each One. They are heard only by each "alone" by which I mean in the sanctity of the One Heart. We are one heart. We are one mind. Joined in wholeheartedness we are the heaven of the world. We replace bitterness with sweetness. We dwell in the reality of the One Heart, creation's birthplace, birthplace of [T]he [N]ew.

The [N]ew is not that which has always existed. It is not that which can be predicted. It is not that which can be formed and held inviolate. The [N]ew is creation's unfolding love. The [N]ew is love's expression. The [N]ew is the true replacement of the false, illusion's demise, joy birthed amongst sorrow. The [N]ew is yet to be created, One Heart to One Heart.

---

* see *Love*, Book 1 of The Grace Trilogy

† *ACOL* C:I.3

This is a course for the heart. The birthplace of [T]he [N]ew.*

I am sitting amid renewed amazement of the announcements made two decades ago.

Do you recall the circumstances in which this introduction came?

Yes. It was a poignant time. My father-in-law, Ed, had died, and on the night when I received it, I had just walked home from the "after the wake" crowd that had gathered at my in-law's house. I remember wondering if the loud gathering was what my mother-in-law, Katie, needed, as she had an extroverted way. With my introverted, quiet-loving way, I was ready to go . . . and a bit melancholy. Ed was always nice to me and the kids. Coming to a family with three children as I did—well—we weren't always comfortable, and that night, I wished it had been otherwise.

Feeling this in a time of sorrow elevated it to a sort of concentrated yearning for "love and its sweetness," to which Jesus responded. I'm not sure I felt the call when I left the home of my in-laws, but I clearly remember it flooding me the minute I got to my door. Once inside I was compelled to sit down at the dining room table and become ready to receive. I'll never forget the compulsion it was—not to dwell on the situation I'd left, but to be ready to hear, which I then did.

Jesus always made the personal universal:

The mind will speak of love and yet hold the heart prisoner to its new rules, new laws, and still say "this is right" and "this is wrong." It will speak of love and not see its intolerance or judgment. It will speak of love to be helpful and with all sincerity, and yet the very

---

* *ACOL* C:I.11-13

logic that it uses, though new, wounds the heart of the most tender, of those most called to love and its sweetness. "I am wrong to feel the way I do" the tender-hearted says to herself and, convinced that another knows what she does not, covers-over her tenderness with protection.*

We spoke of the "female of the species" alongside the feminine in Memoria. *We named the feminine as "those who recognize cause" . . . Those who see "love held prisoner to old or new rules, laws, or actions" . . . those who have been considered the "weaker of the species, the protected, or the used. Those who see that their sweetness has been a liability."*†

Now, you are here for the feminine rising.

Yet I'm one of those who has continued to see my sweetness as a liability, aren't I?

Yes. You are recalling a time when you covered your tender heart with protection. You were still often radical in your actions, but these actions did not offer the protection for which you hoped. And sometimes this was because you didn't allow your goodness to be seen. You set your tender heart aside when dealing with difficulties, trusting what you "felt" but not feeling free to respond with the compassionate but resilient qualities of your heart.

That's true.

And it was true with your in-laws and their children as well . . . until you cared for Katie as she was dying. That changed you. You were no longer the sheepish second wife in the eyes of the family matriarch. You took her into your heart and she responded in kind.

---

* *ACOL* C:I.3

† *Memoria*, p. 141

You know, Mary, I've been sitting here crying for ten minutes, ever since I typed that last sentence.

I'm with you. And I know you.

Like many, my Mari, you've been recovering. This whole time with me, you have been in recovery, and now you are almost free. You've already reached out to the niece and those nephews you loved as they grew, and have now become close to them again.

The question that remains is whether or not you can let your relationship to A Course of Love *change in the same manner.*

I knew you were going to ask me this as soon as you spoke of Katie in this way.

We talked once before of confidence. Things changed after Katie's death because you knew how much your care meant to her. No one else's opinion mattered.

That's true.

You came to the end of defending yourself.

I guess I did.

Would your difficulties have continued for so long if you had seen the "strength" of your heart? If you had seen your heart as the seat of your will to manifest your calling? How often did you question your "doing" instincts as others called you to just "be"? How often did you feel a need to defend your "actions" even from those who found benefit from what your "actions" provided?

We're talking now of what you know you're meant to do.

It probably doesn't sound right, but I always called it "my work," Mary. It was my "work to do," my vocation, and I knew it. Nothing is ever more satisfying than knowing what is yours to do with such . . . intense certainty.

And you know that now?

Yes. I knew it then too.

Then why did you let anyone cause you doubt? You just said you were sure.

I think I was more sure of "the work" than of myself.

Yes! This is the matter you've needed to realize. This is why we're here. "You" didn't then, and sometimes don't now, hold yourself and your work together as one! You claim to, but you shy away from it. Do you see? Each lovely human needs to bring what they "do" and who they "are" together. I keep walking you through these painful events of your past, not because you are different from your sisters and brothers, but because so many are the same as you.

I want you, and all, to quit feeling different in one way and to celebrate your difference in another. You have been taught to be "the same" in your dismissal of the most precious aspects of yourselves. We have spoken of this as "the personal" but now we expand our view of the personal to the heart at the center of your will to live, to love, and to create from love ... The New. This "will to live, love, and create" is about your very life force, its potency and dynamism. This acceptance "in life" could be a description of Metanoia's revolution. And it's a prerequisite to accepting and entering the atmosphere of the imaginal.

*"From here your life becomes imaginal."**

*Your **"life."** The life of each one who stands open to new knowing will realize the imaginal that can only join them through a life they are living authentically. The imaginal came to you in* A Course of Love *only after you had been "stopped" in your production, and realized how open, vulnerable, and attentive you needed to be to do "what is yours to do."*

---

* *ACOL* C:20.10

This is true for all.

I must ask you now to quit bemoaning the difficulties you reveal to me. Not to quit speaking of them, but to cease your speaking of them with regret. Do you know how long the difficulties of your sisters and brothers have been dismissed? Do you not yet see how eager they are to find, along with you, the will to acknowledge the difficulties—so that they can embrace, rather than dismiss, all that needs to be seen newly? The "all are one" promoted by gurus does not often recognize that "doing what is ours to do" is how each will free her or his Self of the past and open themselves and the future for The New.

Remember that we spoke of betrayal:

First, we recognize that life was betrayed. That new life was denied. We recognize that new life will only make its entrance through the end of denial, the end of betrayal, the emergence of acceptance, and the notice of the necessity of Mirari to true living.

How do you not betray the new life offered? How do you cease to deny new life?

Let us grieve these ways so that we can move on without judgment, with loving remembrance, unencumbered by guilt or the weight of the sadness we rightly feel for ourselves and all who have suffered in our name, all who have suffered so that they can join us in this time that stands before us.*

Remember what Jesus said in his description of our Way of Mary. I'm going to paraphrase a little here, so you understand the full meaning.

---

* *Mirari*, p. 229

He acknowledged that our way is a way of creation, that we are birth mothers offering to all men who embrace the feminine, the opportunity to be part of the birthing, in union and relationship, with The New. They can't do it alone and they can no longer "take" what women have. This isn't like a gift of gold, nor the frankincense and myrrh of the old kings. This is a way of acceptance that comes to those who know who they are, those who are undivided, or in other words, those who are "in unity."

Realize, my daughters and sons of The New, that being in unity naturally occurs when you end the divisions by which you've been living. You will know you have done this when you know union and relationship . . . together. It follows that you attain this same unity when you make peace with the feminine and masculine. To be undivided is always to accept unity. Otherwise, you are accepting separation.

Accepting unity is essential for many reasons, the primary of which is that feminine power can't be used. The outward thrust of the masculine will be contained by this antidote to use. Trust yourselves to know those who are in unity, for it is out of these new relationships of feminine and masculine union—with each other and with all life— that you will create and anchor this new time. In relationships of unity, differences are acknowledged, and divisions ended. Each will be the birthplace, the womb of The New in time, and will express this union.

Let "all" true feelings guide you as you create your own new lives.* **Your own true and undivided lives "are" your creation of The New.**

---

* see *Memoria*, p. 44

Realization of the Revelation

In Metanoia, this movement to The New, this continually evolving story of creation, what arises is an element of you that you don't know you're waiting for, sometimes don't realize when it comes, and about which you know only that you know something new. This newness is not like knowing someone else, or something additional. It's almost like knowing someone new "in you." Someone new who *is* you. This is revolutionary because it sparks that sense of aliveness that makes knowing an event, a happening. This experience affects me tremendously in a way I can't say. But this isn't about pronouncements. What we discover can't be deadened by saying, *"Ah ha! This is what it is."*

All I know is that the new capacities or incapacities that overtake us, cause us to reside in continual "coming to know." It's now my greatest desire (and sometimes fear). I feel certain it's come to be from this revolution, and maybe that is what this revolution of consciousness is all about, and what we've been talking of all along: abiding in continual coming to know.

A NEW GENESIS: TWONESS

For your own sake, and the sake of your sisters and brothers, I want you to see newly what we are about. It is with soulfulness that we are writing "a new first page, a new Genesis."* *The rebirth of a Self of love is your soul's acknowledgement and fellowship, not of the same reality that you once saw, but of one less stable and more fluid. One open to new visions.*

The soul is so akin to the Christ in you. But recognizing what is happening without naming it is even better than giving it a name.

I get that, Holy Mary, because I've realized that what I know becomes "something I know is happening." I'm not sure what, but I'm sure. There's nothing to be sure "about." But I'm sure.

Excellent! Your soul doesn't need names. When you allow the nameless to come forward, you recognize your destiny field and those who populate it along with you. Your soul is bound to "your" freedom, the freedom you need to find your truth in your own way, and to find the companions who will travel the spacious realms of The New with you.

The soul is the home of the imaginal. Its essence is to embrace psychic experience.

The vast inner region of soul holds you "within your experience." Embracing you from within that which "generates" experience, a phenomenon of the co-mingling, incarnate spirit of life arises. Here, there is no longer cause to invent or analyze your reasoning, but to recognize the condition of your soul. To watch as it escapes captivity,

---

* *ACOL* T3:14.14

and often "activity." To observe, as it looks through your eyes, the reanimation of your world and your dreams.

The autonomous enlivened soul remakes everything . . . alive. But the soul does not speak in the language of the literal. The soul is where romantic and image-driven language lives. It is where your unique depth and artistry is found. It is where vision arises.

The womb of the soul is the holder of new life, one that includes imagining far beyond the life you have thought yourself to be living. It is the particular place where a new image of life begins to quicken—to show itself. The womb of the soul is masculine as well as feminine and is the embracer of the life-giving power it has been given, in the way it has been given.

The soul's epiphany is the soul's awakening to The New. [In the New,] each soul fervently embraces its sacred charge, which is New Life.

You are held passionately, as you too are to hold: closely enough to create, loosely enough to share, and boldly enough to love in the same fashion. To love in the same fashion is to Love.

Love is not neutral. It is the page on which you write. It is the canvas to which you apply your attributes of being. Love is the source from which, and on which, your creative nature comes to be expressed and made real in the world. This is what creates a new reality: revealed attributes of Love's Being and Expression.[*]

Your willingness to live in the world as the Christ-Self and your willingness to accept your soul's life in you are two aspects of one whole. Twoness always, my Mari.

---

[*] *Memoria*, p. 71 (paraphrase)

Living into twoness is being in Holy Relationship with everything. It's what we're together to bring about, and that which we continue here. I ask you only to remember that we are a duad, and to listen to our dialogues in a new way. Because you do have to reimagine this. Our talking won't help until you see that you can, and need, to speak of this as what "You" have come to know. There is no need to say, "Mary said." You won't be plagiarizing. You don't have to quote me.

And now all has become quiet. Very quiet.

"Holy Mary," I say, "I've always wondered and worried about this. I want to recognize my own part. I do. I love being a receiver, but I know that in dialogue I have become more than a 'receiver.'"

Receiving is what makes you, and your sisters and brothers, participants in the mystery. Now, Metanoia has remade you as a prophet of and witness to the interior region, readying people for The New. All you really need to be is prepared in yourself. Once you are ready, you create willingness in your sisters and brothers ... effortlessly. You don't have to put on an act. When you are prepared, creation of The New is what happens because you are alive, and living fully, and freely, as who you have remembered that you are. Each one who is experiencing The New is making a difference whether they speak a word of it or not. All you must remember is that "You are who you are," and that "Who you are is necessary for the completion of the universe."*

We are here for Metanoia's great turning, the revolution from which Creation of The New is rising . . .

---

* *ACOL* C:17.1

Epilogue, 2024:
As You Begin to Trust
You Begin to Extend Who You Are

Maybe trust has just started to arise in me, Mother and Brother. And it may have started with my participation in a Course of Love event that was held in Findhorn.*

I've been walking you to a genuine yielding of the past, my daughter. You are almost there. It's all available to you in what your Jesus called The Time of Tenderness:

Through receptivity, what your mind finds difficult to accept, your heart accepts with ease. Now you are ready to question what you must. Now you are ready to hear the answer that arises in your own heart or from the voice of the man or woman sitting next to you. Now you are ready to hear all the voices around you without judgment, to enter discussion without an agenda to attend to, to not be so anxious to say what you are thinking that you forget to listen. Now you are ready to let understanding come without the aggressiveness of going out to get it.

You are patient, loving, and kind. You have entered the time of tenderness. You begin to hear what your feelings are saying to you without the interferences and cautions of your thinking mind. You

---

* I was invited to join (via Zoom) the Course of Love event in Findhorn where over thirty diverse people from around the world gathered, under the care of Rodrigo and Budie Cayres. Being with them, and the sincere participants, was powerful enough—even virtually—that I could feel nothing other than love being shared. It was like a perfect ending to a decades long misunderstanding. And all is well.

begin to trust and as you begin to trust you begin to extend who you are. True giving and receiving as one has begun. You have entered Holy Relationship.*

Holy Relationship has always been my greatest desire and fondest of memories: entering holy relationship with you and with friends.

And in order to retain this desire, you have begun to practice forgiveness. Which means you are beginning to leave the past in the past, even though it hasn't felt like it until just this minute. My daughter, you have not been ready, until now, to set the pains of the past aside. Your posture has been one of carefully concealing and managing old hurts, and hadn't yet yielded to a new hope.

It's the combination isn't it, Mother? The combination of completing this work with you and Michael, and the conclusion of leaving behind the old. And it's happening alongside the one-year anniversary of my son Ian's death.† I can now acknowledge "my" new life . . . as well as "his." The Findhorn event was like a reconciling, although I can't say precisely why it felt that way . . . other than, perhaps, that my son's death had changed me.

Mari, my daughter, you just needed an excuse—or an opportunity—to let the old go . . . not despite the postures those in power held . . . but because the postures of the powerful were shown to have changed.

"Mari, my sister," Jesus says, "**The old 'positioning' has yielded to a new hope, a new sincerity. All share the desire now to hold the love given in *A Course of Love*, as closely and as**

---

* *ACOL* A:13-14
† James Ian Mulvaney, 6/18/73 - 11/25/23

intimately as possible . . . and to know that the closest possible love comes in the form of each other. What you felt, joining the group in Findhorn, even from your own home, was . . . Love! That was it. That was all. It is by feeling and acknowledging love that our Course transcends the idea of a "course of learning" and genuinely becomes "A Course of Love."

"Mari, my daughter," Mary says, *"You can truly rest now. There is no disingenuous dynamic to be feared or featured. No agent or issue to dispute. Reconciliation has occurred. A quiet stillness extends.*

"Your Course of Love has come home to rest within you in equal measure to the way in which it extends into the world."

Jesus speaks again. **"With the completion of this work, you carry the Way of the Marys out of your 'receiving' room, into New Life . . . as my Mother once received me in her womb and gave life to me. For the sake of our Selves, as well as your son and all beloveds, we share in the conception, the passion, and the resurrection to New Life. With Love."**

"Always with Love," Mary says.

To which I say, "I will Love you all the days of my life, and beyond, as I will love my son." He has offered me new life, as you and Jesus have offered me new life . . . truer life. Life with you.

DEDICATION

James Ian Mulvaney | June 18, 1973 – November 25, 2023

This book is dedicated, with love, to my son, James Ian Mulvaney. He died last year. My husband Donny and I, along with our daughters and larger family, were badly shaken, and still grieve.

We called him by his middle name, Ian. He was 50 years old and single. He is also survived by his Navy comrade Rasheed R. Rambaran.

Since his death, I found him to be with me more than he was in life... and it felt... wrong, inaccurate. But as I write this, I've come to some peace with it, because I know that, when the sorrow leaves, the "him" that he really was will remain palpable and sustain me and all who loved him.

It took me a while, but I did finally name the trait he carried from little guy to mature man—it was enthusiasm.

I remember saying, when he was little, "He can hardly contain himself!" Enthusiasm was the boyish quality he never lost. I only recently looked at the word more closely, and was surprised to find one of its meanings is "inspired by a god." I thought, "He would have liked that."

My hope is that some of that inspiration might be offered to the grieving in our communities... offered naturally. I don't believe a grief ministry could be organized and remain sincere. But our individual offerings of comfort can express the Way of the Marys and would be a fine ministry for us to embrace. We could recognize new life in the making, without forgetting the life that was or those who may need comfort. Call a friend. Send a card. Respond sincerely. One caring response begets another. That's our magnificent humanity and divinity working as one.

Answers to My Prayers and Gratitude for My People

Great thankfulness fills me as I conclude *Metanoia*.

As I do so, I ponder the relationship between message and messenger, writer and editor, heavenly guardians and spiritual reality, the eternal and the ever-changing. And I'm glad there are no answers. I never thought I'd say that!

The interesting thing is that, if there were stock answers, they'd apply to every category of writing. The relationship of the writer to the written would be fixed. But all writing is not the same. The receptive type of writing that I do began when I was forty-years-old, with *A Course of Love*. Today, at seventy I'm concluding the *Way of the Marys* trilogy. It has been a journey of transformation, of realizing a new form of relationship between myself, the spiritual realm, and the written word.

M

I had a time of despairing and thinking that *Metanoia* would never get done. (It's been over three years.) And when you feel that way, you become profoundly anxious and deeply devoted, both at once. You feel miserable and elated. You are a perfect dichotomy, to yourself and others.

But I'm lucky. My board for the Center for A Course of Love remained steady. Michael Mark always seemed to answer that creative call just before it became an alarm. Christie Lord encouraged me as she marveled over the work as we talked as friends (and more than friends) every day or so. Mike DiConti took care of those important fiscal and practical matters that kept us grounded financially, and Mary Love, (not a board member but closest of friends), comforted me when I doubted or grew weary, knowing what it's like from the depth of her own experience.

It wasn't the content, or Mother Mary, or Jesus, who made it such a different experience. It was me. I've begun to "give in" and not push myself to extremes. Things that were once akin to a fun or interesting challenge aren't so appealing any longer. And I knew I was awaiting something analogous to "my own timing" or even the sense of "our togetherness" in creation of The New. And it is emerging from the divine feminine. I love it that I've found in Michael a creative equal who endlessly inspires me to my best, simply from his own way of being . . . and then assists me in manifesting that "best." I hope I can do the same for him someday. I've been stunned with this volume of the Mary trilogy, and feel blessed with having such a deeply loyal "writer friend."

At the same time, now that the book is finished, it really doesn't feel that it's been unnervingly long in getting here! The route we took no longer matters and I'm thankful and cherish my fellow writers in a whole new way with each creation completed. I also feel great thankfulness for those my age and older who show me the grace of it all, and those younger who show me who I was such a short time ago. In these companions I find the whole cycle of life.

Still, little things have become big—like Michael (who is about 20 years younger than me) telling me, "Hold on to what matters." Like my grandson Henry graduating from high school and deciding to give his energy to becoming a strong and faithful Marine.

No matter the situations arising, I'm beginning to see the potentiality of this time, its grace, the idea of ease, and of not rushing anything. Not pushing myself or anyone else feels particularly good. It could be a consistent way of being if I can let it be. The thing is, though, that when I'm writing, I'm often not doing anything else. And I like it. I wonder now if I can be "more" of a writer pure and simple.

Because there's also a wafting scent of freedom I've never experienced before. While freedom is terrifically important to me, it means something different than it once did. Although I'm not inclined to answer the question of "what" is different, I like that it just doesn't feel as important as it used to, to be able to "do" everything I used to do, and certainly not necessary to do it all by myself!

I've had the privilege of finding this out by working with Michael (as I also did to a lesser extent with *Mirari* and *Memoria*). It wasn't as easy this time, but it wasn't awful either. What I'm liking the most of this long endeavor is the wonder that "help" feels to be—not only from others to me but from me to others. There seems to be a gentle and non-judgmental time being played out, and I feel certain our Holy Ones won't abandon us as we face new challenges, whatever they may be.

Fr. Adrian's death in 2024, was almost as tough on me as was my son's passing in 2023. Father Adrian was my spiritual Father for 30 years, the elder always there, the man who helped me bury my son and my mother, father and brother. A man who, as he gave up most of his priestly duties in his last months asked to visit with my grandson Henry a time or two. That meant the world to me (and I know that Father knew it would).

I can hardly bear to go to Mass at the parish over which he presided without him there, but that's the cycle of life I've entered in a way that seems "all of a sudden" but that has, in truth, been catching up to me for a while. If we're lucky, we all get to this age that can't help but rifle us with frequent occurrences of death and new life.

I'm feeling quite happily done with some aspects of my old life though, and unreservedly engaged by a sense of promise in the years ahead, even while realizing they will not be at all the same.

At whatever juncture you are encountering in your life, I know we can still stand together. Those of us who love *ACIM*, *ACOL*, and the *Way of Mary* have a profound connection in which we can be grateful to each other and united in love and the possibilities that have opened to us. And we don't need to organize to do it. A different time, a time of freedom and The New is upon us.

Somehow, my friends on the Board of The Center for A Course of Love—Michael, Christie, and Mike—make this all seem restful, and not an end of being creative beings . . . just the end of doing it alone.

The best may be yet to come.

Reference Guide and Related Works

References to quotes from *A Course of Love*:

The Course (C)
The Treatises (T) (as there are four treatises, they are related as: T1, T2, T3, and T4)
The Dialogues (D) (as there are both Chapters and Days, you will see: D:1 as well as D:Day1)

The references follow book, chapter and verse.
For example: C:2.1 signifies The Course, Chapter 2, Verse 1.

You will find this same order in regard to the other books of *A Course of Love's* Combined Volume. For example: T1:2.1, T2:2.1, T3:2.1, T4:2.1 signify Chapter 2, Verse 1 of each of the four treatises.

References to paragraphs within the Epilogue or the Addendum may be referenced simply as, for example, E.6 or A.4.

RELATED WORKS BY MARI PERRON

Memoria: The Way of the Marys (2022)
Memoria continues the intimate personal sharing between Mari Perron and Mary of Nazareth that was begun in *Mirari: The Way of the Marys*. Together as one, yet distinct of voice, this beautiful duad

explores the importance of balancing the divine masculine with the divine feminine and of remembering what is to come through the power of Memoria. The dialogue Mari and Holy Mary share is a deeply personal one, but also universal. Prevalent issues of our time are discussed, including gender identification, personal empowerment, and the burden of senseless choices that smother true freedom. Mari and Mary share scenes from their lives filled with uncertainty, devotion, and wonder. The ordinary and the miraculous merge, and the means to live as we truly are is discovered, along with the power this offers.

Mirari: The Way of the Marys (2020)

Mary of Nazareth reveals herself as a powerful advocate for the living. Beginning with a potent, archetypal scene, she calls women to both creation and protection of the "new babe" who is . . . "us." It is through union: union of the feminine and masculine and union of the earthly and celestial realms that The New will be created. In this first of a three-book series, Mary of Nazareth gives expression to the fullness and the power of the divine feminine, and the innate ways of being and knowing that women and men can bring to a wounded world. She invites a time of grief even while "Mirari" means "wonder," a wonder that is to be found in the call to create "The New."

A Course of Love

Three books: The Course, The Treatises, and The Dialogues, first published in single volumes beginning in 2001. Republished in a Combined Volume in 2014 by Take Heart Publications.

Received from Jesus, The Course, The Treatises and The Dialogues are arranged in such a way that they guide us from who we thought we were to who we truly are. In this movement, learning is left behind as we enter new ways of knowing and being. This way of the heart dwells within us. The heart's memories are called upon for creation of The New. Dialogue is revealed as a new means of coming to know and being known, and the Way of Mary is introduced for the first time.

The Given Self: Recovering Your True Nature (2009)

In this most personal of Mari Perron's works, she shares from her ordinary life as the event of her dad's death and the birth of her first grandson occur within weeks of each other. With grief and joy intermingled, her exploration ranges from the ordinary to the sublime to the practical. As she comes to embrace her authentic self, she draws from her humanity, her memories, her loneliness, and from mystical experiences, revealing that they are all of one piece and that none remain neat or orderly.

Creation of the New (2007)

This mystical experience has relevance to this new work, especially due to its vision, language, and imagery. It came from what Perron feels is her "own" mystical voice, to announce The New.

The Grace Trilogy (1997)

The trilogy includes:

Love: A Story of Connection by Mari Perron, Julieanne Carver, and Mary Kathryn Love

Grace: Finding the Light by Mary Kathryn Love, and

Peace: Meeting at the Threshold by Mari Perron.

Love shares the story of the experiences of three close friends and workmates who, together, "felt into" new ways of knowing, being and sharing. Their profound experiences occurred with each other and with angels.

Mary Love's *Grace* is a personal, profound and tender experience of grace and new life.

In *Peace*, Mari connects with an angel and experiences her initial encounter with otherworldly realms. She discovers their enduring wisdom, shared in companionship.

Mari shares:
In rereading the Trilogy recently, I was so grateful for that miraculous time being captured when it was. It is always a wonder when a book transcends the time in which it was written. While *Love* is available as an e-book, the three paperback editions of *Love*, *Grace* and *Peace* are out of print.

ONLINE RESOURCES

The Way of Mary: www.wayofmary.com
The Way of Mary extends the reach of Mary's words into today's world. A search facility enables further exploration, as do selected quotes and reviews.

Mari Perron: www.mariperron.com
On this website, Mari's focus is on exploring the breadth and depth of the "new way" that we experience after we live into the message of *A Course of Love*. She also offers Musings (a blog) and The Jesus Chronicles, never before published conversations with Jesus.

A Course of Love: www.acourseoflove.org
A Course of Love is the major theme here. Many resources and possibilities for connection are noted. You can find more on Mari Perron's experiences and vision from the "Mari Perron" tab via the "Home" page.

You may also see Mari's videos about *A Course of Love* and life on YouTube at www.youtube.com/c/MariPerron/videos.

Course in Miracles Society: www.cimsmiracles.com
I feel it's also important to recognize the Course in Miracles Society and their publication of *ACIM*'s *Original Edition*. I think of it often because I know how important it is to have these unaltered editions available. In addition, CIMS has always embraced *A Course of Love*. They believe *ACOL* is a continuation of *ACIM OE* as well as a beautiful gift.

THE CENTER FOR A COURSE OF LOVE

The Center for a Course of Love: www.centerforacourseoflove.com
The Center's focus comes from the model given in The Dialogues: Attending to "the dawning of the consciousness of unity . . . a state

that cannot be learned . . . only revealed to you through unity and relationship." (*ACOL* T4:12.25)

Mari hopes that you let *A Course of Love* embrace you in a way that invites you to be and to create The New. *ACOL*, read in love and wholeheartedness, can propel you into a future different than the past.

The Center for A Course of Love holds the copyright and Trademark for *A Course of Love* for the hopeful reason of embracing a new way of knowing, being and creating . . . with love and wholeheartedness. Part of this is going forward newly and part letting go of the past.

The Center offers two search facilities. One, "Discover ACOL," will be helpful for those who would like to easily find the context of any of the quotes from *A Course of Love* that are referenced in The Way of Mary series. Another is "Cocreate ACIM OE/ACOL," a combined tool for searching *ACOL* and the wonderful *ACIM OE* (Original Edition) simultaneously. Similar search facilities for The Way of Mary books are available at The Way of Mary website noted above.

Dialogue videos with readers and friends:
www.centerforacourseoflove.org/dialogue/

The Center for A Course of Love is a 501(c) nonprofit. The Center, and Mari Perron, gratefully accept your gifts.
www.centerforacourseoflove.org/ways-to-give/

SPREAD THE WORD

Amazon Reviews:

A great gift you can give to an author as a grateful reader is to rate and review their work on Amazon. This makes a lasting contribution to sales, the ability of the work to reach those who are looking for it . . . and supports the author too. Please consider reviewing all of the Way of Mary books. Thank you!

www.ingramcontent.com/pod-product-compliance
Lightning Source LLC
Chambersburg PA
CBHW032029290426
44110CB00012B/730